A Footpath in the Wilderness:
The Early Days of PATC

Carol Niedzaliek, Editor

First Edition

Edited by Carol Niedzaliek, PATC Archivist,
with assistance from Aaron Watkins, PATC Publications Chair,
in celebration of the 75th Anniversary of PATC

Typists: Rita Bauman, Sarah Brion, Dede Pitts, and Sujit Ray

Published by
Potomac Appalachian Trail Club
Publications Committee
118 Park Street, S.E.
Vienna, VA 22180

A footpath in the wilderness : the early days of PATC / Carol
Niedzaliek, editor.— 1st ed.
    p. cm.
 ISBN 0-915746-93-X
 1. Potomac Appalachian Trail Club—History. I. Niedzaliek,
Carol.
 GV199.42.A68 F66 2003
 917.5—dc22

                          2003016515

Contents

Foreword

Carol Niedzialek
PATC Archivist
2003

As archivist, I received several requests for information, and in searching through material I came across old articles which I couldn't help but read. Reading these articles, I realized that these stories about the early days of PATC are like time capsules put away 75 years ago.

Most of the stories contained in this book were written and published in the *PATC Bulletin* in the decades of the 1930's and 1940's. Others are written at later times, but reflect on activities in the 1920's, 1930's and 1940's. In these stories, we make acquaintance with our founding fathers. Personalities far removed from our time are brought to life. Myron Avery was the first club president, Frank Schairer the first supervisor of trails, Harold Allen the editor of PATC's first guidebook, *Guide to Footpaths in the Blue Ridge*, Jean Stephenson was PATC's historian, who later founded the ATC monthly magazine *Appalachian Trailway News*. Other authors were very active members of the club. Another intention of this book is to present an idea of what it took to get the trail up and going, and reveal what the club members were doing and what interested them. In MacKaye's words, it is the "first chapter in a long story." The interview with George Corbin in 1969 is precious and gives a glimpse of mountaineer life in the 1920's and 1930's.

The title of this book was taken from Frank Schairer's story. Some articles are short and some are long, enabling a reader to choose whatever one has time for. I hope that readers will enjoy these stories. They should give a broad picture of how the club started out and then flourished.

I am ever so grateful to club members Rita Bauman, Sarah Brion, Dede Pitts, and Sujit Ray who helped with keyboarding these articles. Their help saved immense time.

PATC History

Myron Avery, pointing with axe, late 1930's. From left: Howard Olmstead, Bob Beach, Dr. Schmeckbeir, Mary Jo Williams, Avery

In the Very Beginning

by Myron H. Avery
July 1942

With the Appalachian Trail initially completed in 1937 and the Appalachian Trail Conference with its functioning and contributions to Trail technique so generally known, it perhaps would be of interest to roll back the pages of time for two decades. What were trail conditions in 1920? What trail systems were then available? What was there in the way of guidebooks and literature of the Trail?

Two decades have exacted a heavy toll from the ranks of those who might, from their personal participation in trail building, have narrated in detail this background of the Appalachian Trail and its origin. Most Trail users, with some vagueness, can say that it was a proposal published in some magazine with a restricted circulation in 1921 or 1922, announced by Benton MacKaye of Shirley, Massachusetts. The factors which made such a proposal particularly opportune and made it logical that it should be advanced in 1921 are, however, obscured.

As the history is reviewed, one fact impresses. The year of 1920 was a definite milestone in Trail history. It marked the advance, the receding of the frontier of the "hiker's terrain." Beyond New England and New York City in 1920, there were none of the hiking clubs or groups which exist today. The great Appalachian, Allegheny, and Blue Ridge chains were an unknown land. There was a very definite lack of accurate knowledge of the limits of the Appalachian Range and of its pattern. This is reflected in the originally suggested termini of the Appalachian Trail: Mt. Washington in the north and Mt. Mitchell in the south. It is further emphasized by the search for the southern terminus of the Trail route, which was not finally determined until 1929.

In 1920, trails and trail opportunities were practically synonymous with the White Mountains of New Hampshire. Here, for half a century, pioneers in the Appalachian Mountain Club and others had developed an extensive system of trails. This, however, was far from any concept of a through route. It was a series of trails to the outstanding features of a roughly rectangular mountainous region.

The other area where trail interest was manifest before 1920 was to the west along the crest of the Green Mountains. This project had more the element of the through trail, since it was projected to extend the length of Vermont. Undoubtedly, its nature has inspired other extensive through trail systems. Since 1910, the Green Mountain Club of Vermont had been at work on what ultimately became the 257-mile Long Trail, extending the length of Vermont from Canada to Massachusetts. What an inventory in 1919 would have disclosed as to the extent of the completed trail system in Vermont, perhaps some pioneer member of the Green Mountain Club can say.

Benton MacKaye, early 1930's

By 1920, the New England Trail Conference had been in existence for four years. It was endeavoring to encourage trail construction and to connect areas where trails existed with trailless areas, now much frequented. At the early meetings of this Conference, there were advanced several proposals of extensive through systems, none, however, as ambitious as the Appalachian Trail project. The records of these meeting do much to portray the background of the land of trails.

There was a second factor in this development of interest in through trail systems which dates to 1920. Attention was becoming focused on the Palisades Interstate Park area. Its officials, particularly Major William A. Welch, General Manager of the Park, sought to utilize these opportunities through the volunteered development of trails by the hiking clubs in the vicinity of New York City. So, in 1920, a trail crept east across the Palisades Interstate Park. First known as the Tuxedo-Tom Jones Trail, it is today the Ramapo-Dunderberg Trail, the oldest maintained and marked trail in the Park. The through Appalachian Trail uses a portion of this R-D Trail, as it is generally known.

Thus, to coordinate this increasing volunteer trail work, instigated by Major Welch, there came into existence the Palisades Trail Conference. Later it was reorganized as the present-day New York-New Jersey Trail Conference. Until his death in 1938, Raymond H. Torrey was the directing force in this group. For many years Mr. Torrey contributed to the *New York Post* a column, "The Long Brown Path." These articles form an invaluable treasury of knowledge of this area, its geography, history, geology, botany, and kindred subjects. It is also a valuable record of progress in trail building prior to the records of the Appalachian Trail. These date from 1925, when Arthur Perkins of Hartford, Connecticut, resurrected what had become a moribund project.

Fortunately, Frank Place of the New York–New Jersey Trail Conference has maintained a set of scrapbooks of "The Long Brown Path" articles. It is a unique collection. With an antiquary's interest, there is a tendency to digress over long in this record between 1918 and 1925, but we are concerned here with the records of such happenings that portray the beginnings of the AT project.

The germs of a developing through trail project are noted in Mr. Torrey's report in "The Long Brown Path" of December 16, 1921, of the meeting of the New England Trail Conference. The specific proposal was that advanced by J. Ashton Allis, long-term member of the Appalachian and Green Mountain Clubs. The proposal, in part, was:

"Seventeen hundred miles of trails, mostly in New Hampshire, Maine, and Vermont, were reported to be open to hikers, at the annual meeting of the New England Trail Conference in Boston last Friday and Saturday. These trails number 447, 25 being bridle paths totalling 46 miles, 60 graded paths totalling 175 miles, 17 'spotted' paths totalling 29 miles, leaving 373 'cleared' trails, of the type used by most hikers, totalling 1,433 miles..."

We Had Some Marvelous Times in the Old Days

An "Interview" with J. F. Schairer, Supervisor of Trails
October 1942

"We had some marvelous times in the Trail Club in the old days. It's only when you have some trouble and difficulty in doing things, as you are having now, that you really appreciate them. When you get a trip down to the mountains now, you really do appreciate it. You no longer feel it's a place you can go just any week you please. Now you can go only occasionally, drive along at 30 miles per hour, but you enjoy the country on the way. I will never forget our first trip to the Blue Ridge.

Frank Schairer (center) with PATC members,
circa 1930

"The way I got into the Trail Club was this. I joined the Wild-flower Society through a friend in the Department of Agriculture and there I met Andy [H. C. Anderson] and Dr. P. L. Ricker and a whole bunch. We used to go on camping trips in the Catoctins and so on. They moved so slowly though, looking at flowers, that they didn't cover much territory. Ricker one day said to me, "They are thinking of forming a trail club. Would you he interested?' I said I would. A few days later, November 22, 1927, we went down to Andy's office in the Metropolitan Bank Building for a meeting. Myron Avery was there, Dr. Schmeckebier and Myron's uncle, the late Judge Joseph Cox, P. L. Ricker and Homer Corson. We decided to form a trail club and discussed what to call it. I remember I held out for 'Blue Ridge Appalachian Trail Club.' We compromised on 'Potomac' as that name covered the area we expected to work in. Myron was to act as president, Dr. Ricker was vice-president, Andy was secretary and Schairer was treasurer, and if there ever was a lousy treasurer it was one J. F. Schairer. The auditing committee two years later audited the books. They said, 'The treasurer's accounts are in order but he keeps no books.' So Myron got the brilliant idea that more orthodox accounting methods were needed and that Marian Lapp would be the girl for the job. He said to me, 'We will create a new office and you will be the Supervisor of Trails.' So that's how that happened.

"In any case, a week or two before this meeting to form the club, Andy called me and said there was a fellow named Avery and Judge Cox and that the four of us would go to the mountains. We would take the Paris bus and Andy and I would go south and Myron and Judge Cox would go north. (This was in October 1928.) Then we would report on how the situation was, how hard it would be to cut a trail. None of us knew anything about it and we had a terrible time finding our way. Andy and I had a topographic map, a lot of ambition, and lunch. Anyway, when we got together again, Andy and I reported that it was going to be a tough job to cut a trail. Myron and Judge Cox said there would be nothing to it. They had old wood roads; we didn't. Incidentally, it took several months of weekends to get even a narrow trail cut.

"Then the problem was that we had just that small group. The only people who had any interest in the Trail were people from New England, and no one else knew anything about the Trail. That is where Schmeckebier knew it and he had taken part away back in 1922 in meetings in Washington when Benton MacKaye as Field Manager was trying to get the AT going. Myron had just come down to Washington after a year and a half at Hartford, Connecticut, where he had been closely associated with Arthur Perkins. Judge Perkins was Chairman of the Trail Conference and was beginning to revive the project after two or three years of inactivity. Thus our interest in Washington fortunately coincided with the time when Judge Perkins was beginning to get things going again on the AT in other places. He soon came down to encourage us.

"So, the nucleus we had to start with was from the Wildflower Society. Charlie Thomas used to lead wildflower trips. Actually, Myron, Andy, Charlie Thomas and I did a large part of the work. Ricker had wildflower things to do. Nobody had any cars, and try and persuade somebody to go to the mountains on those terrible Virginia roads! They thought we were crazy to go down and work all day for nothing and said nobody would ever use the trails we cut anyway.

"The thing which no one today can understand is how really difficult it was back in 1928 to get to the Blue Ridge and how much of an unknown land it was. Nobody knew anything about it except around Skyland.

"So that's what we were up against that first year. The only active hiking club in Washington was the Red Triangle Club, and they went in largely for Sunday afternoon hikes. Once a year they scheduled a hike from Bluemont to Harpers Ferry and always had a dance at the little hotel at Bluemont. There was no continuous trail on the mountain. We wanted to convince them that the Appalachian Trail was a going thing. Our objective was to get the Trail from Bluemont all the way to Harpers Ferry done in time to schedule a Red Triangle hike over it in the spring.

"On our first real work trip, Andy, Myron and I took a train to Harpers Ferry. There was a bridge across in those days. We had to learn from sad experience how canteens are needed in the Blue Ridge, and we didn't have the kind of tools used today, clippers and weeders. We learned our trail technique the hard way. We used, that day, mainly Boy Scout axes. We were all dying of thirst after getting to the top. It took us all day to get from south of Chimney Rock to a point about half mile beyond. Our axes got so dull we couldn't cut with them. We just had to saw off the twigs. When it came to Trail markers, we had a few copper ones that Major Welch had made at Bear Mountain and had given to us as his contribution to getting started. Ricker's idea was that we needed something to mark turns, so we bought those little wooden garden labels, little slats an inch wide and a foot and a half long or so. Ricker printed on them 'Appalachian Trail' or 'Spring' or 'Viewpoint.' They solved the problem of marking the turns. I guess there may be a relic or two left in the Club stuff as a reminder of the old days.

"So we started the work trips to Harpers Ferry, going by train and staying at a place called Himes Cottage. We would go on Saturday afternoon and would get up at five in the morning. The trouble was that we only had three or four workers and they were all inexperienced. After the first trip, we got to using pruning shears. Each fellow had to buy his tool. The Club hadn't any money to buy tools.

"Anyway, we kept pushing the Trail, and we had to pick old wood roads and faint mountain paths. We couldn't pick the perfect route then because it was too tough. Remember, between Harpers Ferry and Bluemont there was at that time no decent road through Keys Gap, only a cart path. You could get up on the west side, but you had to have a high-hung car. Just to show how difficult it was: You had to go to Harpers Ferry, drive quite a distance on a dirt road to Millville, and get a mountaineer out of his cabin to take you across the river by a hand-operated ferry. Finally, you would get to the top of Keys Gap if your car was high hung. If it wasn't, you never got there. You couldn't get up the east side; there was no road through to Charles Town. We worked from both ends, from Bluemont and from Harpers Ferry. I remember one trip in February, we started on Sunday morning, and it was nearly twelve o'clock noon before we arrived at Keys Gap. We were working near the Deer Lick and the Trail was really bad. By the time we walked to the Deer Lick it was three-thirty or a quarter of four, and we figured we had only fifteen minutes to work before we had to start back. It started to sleet and the sole came off my shoe and there I was. We put in fifteen minutes of hard work and had to race to get back to Keys Gap before dark. The Trail was so bad and it took so much time to walk in that we were convinced we couldn't get much work done when we started from Washington on Sunday morning.

"Then I remember that finally somebody persuaded Harold Allen to take his car to the mountains. He was the first man to ever volunteer to do so. Harold, you know, was the first Editor of the *Blue Ridge Guide*. It was an open car and I remember riding in it in February, with the temperature about zero. We drove down to Snickers Gap. The road through the Gap was a winding dirt road. A car could seldom make it in low, but would

Schairer fishing

have to be pushed. On such trips we never got home before midnight.

"The Red Triangle hike was scheduled for some time in March and we had several bad weekends in February that had delayed us. It finally came to the time when the Red Triangle trip was the following Sunday. Andy and I were the trouble-shooters for the last sprint. Our assignment was to get the last two miles of Trail in shape. The Trail followed wood roads beyond Keys Gap and then swung down around the west side of the mountain. It was a faint path, solid with locust briars for two miles. We hedged a little. We got to Keys Gap and walked down to a log cabin and talked to some mountain people, finally persuading them to let a couple of their kids help us the next day. Well, the next day the two boys didn't show up. But they sent two others in their place, and we worked as hard as any four people could. We had two throw out and two cut and then we alternated. We got the two miles done. We paid the fellows fifty cents for the day out of our own pockets. This was big pay for mountain boys; they beamed. The Trail was not beautiful but it was reasonably well marked. The Red Triangle had a trip over it and after that they were convinced that the Appalachian Trail was no myth. Bill Richardson of the Red Triangle joined the Trail Club and has always been a good worker and a genial chap on a camping trip.

"When you take into consideration our transportation difficulties in those days, you will understand that it was a major accomplishment to have completed the Trail from Bluemont to Harpers Ferry in that period from November to March. As I said, it wasn't a beautiful Trail, but you could get through.

"Finally, Andy bought a Chevrolet. Then, every weekend we had transportation. Those first two years I didn't spend a single weekend in Washington, except for one, when I was sick in bed with the flu on Easter Sunday.

"We learned everything the hard way. We had at first never heard of painting blazes. We later found that it was better down here not to cut ax blazes in the wood, and the scraper system was gradually developed.

"To show you the development of the overseer system: We found out that the Trail always got bad again, and so we started the general idea of the overseer system in the sense that the officers and the few members divided up the Trail among them. Walter Jex, a stalwart worker for P. E. P. Co., used to get out a lot and he could really put in a day's work. He had the section from Harpers Ferry to Bluemont, and when a man has 18 miles to take care of, you can figure that he must really work.

"The goal was to prove to people in Washington that this crest Trail could be followed without going off the mountain. The next objective (Myron always had 'objectives') was to try and get the Trail through to Linden by November, the end of the first year of the Club's existence. Well, it's a long way from Snickers Gap to Linden and we got busy. By then it wasn't quite so bad because we had proved that the Trail wasn't a foolish idea and we began to get new people interested. There were Charlie Thomas and Herman Nolte and so on. We had maybe 25 or 40 instead of 6 or 8, and that number really made an impression on the Trail. In those days members either worked or didn't come out again.

"At the end of the first year, we had completed 42 miles of Appalachian Trail from Harpers Ferry to Linden. So that, I think, covers the early story of the first year. This was in 1928 and 1929. From then on, it was a case of pushing the project forward.

"Even today, the easiest way to get to the Trail is to take a train to Harpers Ferry. We are now back in almost the same situation in which we found ourselves at the very beginning. Because Harpers Ferry is the most convenient point of contact with the Trail and because many people get their first impression of the Trail there, it is particularly important that it should be kept in good shape in that area.

"However, our situation today is in some respects a great deal better because we have decent roads. Let's just go over the road situation in the early days. I have already pointed out that you could get to Keys Gap from the West Virginia side, but it took most of the day. It was a terrible road that could only be negotiated in a high-hung car, and then there was the problem of the Millville ferry. The road on the Virginia, or east, side was impossible.

"Let's just follow down the Trail route. There was a road through Snickers Gap, but it was dirt and rough as the very devil. The road from Snickers Gap to Mount Weather was just about passable. The only good road (and we thought it was a wonderful road) was the one from Washington to Winchester, passing through Ashby Gap. Manassas Gap? It was worth your life to go through to Manassas Gap! In those days every stream had to be forded, even on the road to Winchester. The only way to get to Manassas Gap was to go through on what is now U. S. 50 to Boyce, then to White Post, take a road from White Post to Front Royal, and then drive 8 miles from Front Royal to Linden. If you tried to come in to Linden from the east, you were sure to get stuck.

"There was a road through Chester Gap, a narrow, asphalt one, only wide enough for one car. We did go in that way, but it wasn't practical. We used to drive up from Flint Hill into Smoot's place, a mountaineer's cabin at the foot of Mount Marshall. In the early days we had a good many trips there. That is how the Applesauce House got its name. It was an abandoned mountaineer's cabin. We had a Trail Club camping trip there and Charlie Thomas was to bring the coffee. He brought everything but the coffee. He brought the cream, the sugar, and the pot to make it in, but no coffee. It was in the fall and there was a big apple orchard near the abandoned cabin, so everybody picked up apples. The girls peeled them and made applesauce with the sugar Charlie had brought. Everybody referred to the cabin after that as the Applesauce House.

"One of the worst problems was cutting the Trail from the Applesauce House to the top of Mount Marshall. It was our first attempt at building brand new trail where there wasn't even a sign of a rabbit path. Didn't we sweat over that Mount Marshall! As we were cutting south, we used to drive in from Little Washington and camp at the head of Harris Hollow. There was a wood road leading 1.8 mi. to Gravelly Spring. We either camped at the foot or came in at night and camped at Gravelly Spring. We would work both ways from Gravelly Spring.

"When we went to build the Trail further down, they were just laying the paved road from Sperryville to Luray over Panorama. The old road was full of rocks and boulders and so steep that we had to push on the steep grades. So, it was a major problem to get to Panorama.

"Now Fishers Gap: we never got in from the east except one time and then we had to practically build the road. Fishers Gap was always called 'The Red Gate' because at the top of the mountain there was a pasture and a prominent red gate. You could always get to Fishers Gap from Stanley, near Luray, but we never got there from the east side except that one time as a stunt.

"The next place was at Swift Run Gap and that was a little, narrow, dirt road, very bumpy. It was a major undertaking to take a car there. And, of course, it took a long time to get down there. Unless you could go down for two or three days, it wasn't worthwhile to go.

"The trouble with that Southern Shenandoah country was that we couldn't get anybody to go down. I remember we had a three-day weekend down there one time to scout and mark a route. Myron and I left Washington and went down by train to Luray, where we hired Emerson, who was a taxi man in Luray, for the sum of five dollars to get us from Luray down through Stanley to the red gate at Fishers Gap. Myron and I started out from that point, zigzagging all over the mountain. Our knowledge of the country was drawn from some notes made in 1922 by Dr. H. S. Hedges of Charlottesville, when he was scouting for the AT in that region. They helped a lot. We camped that first night at the old Spanish oak, which is roughly half a mile southwest of the point where Pocosin Shelter now is. This was the locality of a gruesome mountain murder, but after carrying trail clearing tools and food and other necessities for three days we were not staying awake to see ghosts.

"The second night we arrived back from Swift Run Gap at dusk, with a thundershower coming up, at Jesse Lamb's cabin on the west slope of Bear Fence Mountain. We set up our tent in his yard. The next morning we started out in a light snow. There were bear tracks in the snow at the foot of Bear Fence Mountain and that impressed both of us because we thought the bear stories we had heard were fairy tales. Finally, the third day, we got back to the Red Gate, having scouted and marked the Appalachian Trail from Fishers Gap to Swift Run in those three days. We had found lots of wood roads. We had to walk to Stanley and call Luray to get Emerson to come and pick us up.

"We figured we walked 55 miles on that trip, and it was real work. I won't forget sliding down the mud road from Fishers Gap to Stanley in a heavy rainstorm. I wonder if any PATC member has ever gone to the AT via Luray and Stanley on the railroad?

"To sum up the thing: The roads were bad in the old days. Nobody wanted to go because they thought the Trail Club people were a bunch of freaks. It was hard to get to the Trail; we often spent the whole day getting there, with only an hour or two to work. We are in almost the same situation today. The roads aren't so bad, but it is hard to get to the Trail. However, the same determination that saw the gang through in cutting the Trail in the early days will see the Appalachian Trail maintained today, perhaps in not quite the same high standard, but at least it will be well marked and reasonably cleared. it will be a path through the wilderness, possibly not quite as wide as it was at one time, but still a path through the wilderness. It is up to everybody nowadays to realize the situation, step right into things, and they will get as much pleasure out of trips to the mountains as we did in the early days. Things that are difficult to do are more desirable."

PATC Bulletin #2

Anonymous
April 1928

For the benefit of the members of the Club who have not been able to take part in the trail cutting expeditions, perhaps it will be desirable to review the work done by the Club. The Club began work in November, 1927, with a meeting of a group of six interested people at Mr. Anderson's office. At the second meeting, on November 22nd, the present organization was effected. The membership of the Club is now 39. Since November, practically every weekend has seen some work done on the Trail, either in the way of scouting or tail cutting. The largest party at any time was 10 with three cars. As a record of our achievement, we point to a continuous stretch of Standard Trail along the Blue Ridge from Harpers Ferry south to Linden, a distance of between 45 and 50 miles. The through hike over all this section, which is scheduled for April 13-15, is to demonstrate the existence of this continuous trail. At this time, the Trail will be measured by the use of a measuring wheel, and guidebook data for this section will then be printed and sent to each member of the Club. With these data the hiker could dispense with the necessity of having some one familiar with the route go with him as guide and if some marker had been destroyed, he would not be in doubt as to the way.

After its through hike, the Club next plans to cut the section of the Trail between Thornton Gap (Panorama) and Skyland. This is for the purpose of making Skyland and the Shenandoah Park accessible to the hiker from Thornton Gap and avoiding the necessity of the longer route through Luray. In this work, we have the hearty cooperation of Mr. G. Freeman Pollock, the owner of Skyland, a member of the Club. The cutting of this link will conclude the major part of the Trail cutting for the summer, but the Club expects to mark trails and prepare guidebook data for the trails south of Skyland which can be used as a part of the Appalachian Trail. Trips of this nature will be somewhat informal and will be composed of small parties of the more energetic hikers.

With the coming of cool weather in the fall, the Club will recommence trail cutting through the area from Linden to Thornton Gap in order to connect up the two sections already cut. Then it will be a matter of extending the Trail north from Harpers Ferry and south beyond the limit of this summer's work.

The Club hopes that by fall it will have been able to put signs and have prepared trail description on a sufficient area in the Park so that its guidebook sheets, which for the present are being prepared in loose leaf form, will constitute a guidebook to a very considerable section of the Park and to the Blue Ridge north of the Park.

The Mountain Magazine, the official organ of the Associated Outdoor Clubs of America will carry in its April issue an article by Secretary H. C. Anderson on the Club's work. This article is illustrated by a very excellent sketch map prepared by F. E. Matthes, of the United States Geological Survey, a member of the Club. A copy of this issue of the magazine will be mailed to you. The Mountain Magazine carries reports of the work done on the Appalachian Trail and in addition serves to keep us in touch with the other clubs all over the country.

How PATC Sprouted From The Wildflower Preservation Society

Clippings from "The Dogwood's Bark"
by Grant Conway
1929-1932

The story of how the Potomac Appalachian Trail Club grew out of the Washington, D.C. Chapter of the Wildflower Preservation Society was related many times by the late J. Frank Schairer, a charter member of PATC who, like all charter members, was also a member of the WPS.

Frank's passing last September was a sad reminder that the voices who can recite first-hand recollections of the early days of PATC, its origins and its first labors, are growing fewer and weaker. It seems worthwhile, therefore, to try to preserve at least the written recollections of those early, truly pioneering days; when the Appalachian Trail was still largely a vision in the minds of a handful of ardent hikers and nature lovers and when outings were concerned less with trail maintenance then with actual trail cutting.

While the relationship between the Wildflower Society and PATC is well known to the surviving members of the WPS, that relationship is not well documented for the benefit of more recent and future PATCers. The relationship is significant, however; a fact reaffirmed for this writer recently while sorting some of the papers of the late Kathryn Fulkerson and Marian Lapp Otis, early officers of PATC. Among the records and relics preserved by Kathryn and Marian were several "schedules of outings" of the Wildflower Society which include a least a partial genesis of the origins of PATC. In 1927, these schedules were issued under the title of "The Dogwood's Bark."

The aims of the Wildflower Preservation Society were familiar ones, timely even in the 1920's, and stressed conservation of natural resources, especially wild natural areas, and the study of this natural heritage. When the activities of the WPS diminished, including the scope and frequency of outings, following the departure of its foremost guiding spirit, Dr. E. T. Wherry, conservation-minded PATCers in the society provided the leadership for a new organization which would become the Wilderness Society, but that is another story.

What follows are verbatim, more or less, excerpts from surviving copies of "The Dogwood's Bark" saved and preserved by Kathryn and Marian and arranged here chronologically to provide a glimpse of those early days. While the logistics for the outings catalogued in "The Dogwood's Bark" may have a familiar ring to modern-day PATC hikers, bear in mind that in 1928 automobiles and buses were a far cry from the heated, air conditioned, softly-sprung conveyances we enjoy today; that these were the days before the federal-aid interstate highway system, and that magnesium pack frames and rip-stop nylon were still a long way in the future. Here, then, are clippings from:

The Dogwood's Bark
- Outings -

Jan - Feb 1928

This (Wildflower) society, cooperating with other eastern outdoor clubs interested in completing a trail to scenic points along the top of mountain ridges from Mt. Katahdin in Maine to Lookout Mountain in Tennessee and Stone Man Mountain in Georgia to be known as the Appalachian Trail, will join with the local Potomac Appalachian Trail Club in helping to scout out and open up the trail between Gettysburg, Pennsylvania and Stony Man Mountain, Virginia in the proposed Shenandoah National Park, but will still keep up for members desiring short trips the one or two mostly four to six mile trips a month as before. Assistance is, however, desired from members interested in 10 to 12 mile trips for trail cutting, a few cooks for the trail cutters and automobiles for weekend overnight trips. The scenery is superb and as soon as some of the more accessible Virginia portions are opened up, bus trips with short hikes to scenic points will be taken if enough are interested to fill a bus. The spring flowers should be attractive along the trail. Those who took the High Knob trip last year and Catoctin trip this year had only a small sample of the good trips to come.

The Appalachian Trail

Some seven years ago a man in Shirley, Massachusetts, dreamed a dream. He envisioned a long trail for hikers winding its way along the mountain regions of the eastern United States, so long that it reached from Maine to Georgia. This trail approached by branch trails from congested centers, made more available to the city dweller the peace and relaxation of the woods and mountains.

The idea, when first proposed by Benton MacKaye, seemed little more than a dream. Today, hundreds of miles of trails along the proposed route have been cut through and marked, mainly in New York

Myron Avery with measuring wheel,
early 1930's

and New England, and the work in other sections has been seriously undertaken by different groups and organizations.

While plans for carrying the trail along the Blue Ridge of Virginia have been considered by different groups and individuals, practically no work on that section has been done until the organization of the Potomac Appalachian Trail Club this fall (1928). The primary purpose of the Club is the construction and maintenance of the Appalachian Trail and tributaries thereto along the mountain regions most accessible from Washington. Some 50 miles of the trail route have already been scouted, and it is hoped in the near future to start the actual work of cutting through the trail. The section of the trail which the Club has undertaken will eventually extend southward into the proposed Shenandoah National Park and northward to the Pennsylvania line at Pen Mar.

It is no small task which the Club has before it. How long it will take will depend upon the number who are willing to help. All lovers of the woods and mountains are invited to join the club and share in some way in opening up this interesting region to hikers and nature students. The officers of the Club are: M. H. Avery, president; P. L. Ricker, vice-president; J. F. Schairer, treasurer; H. C. Anderson, secretary.

Weekend, January 1-2, 1928
Harper's Ferry

A trip for the purpose of clearing a link on the trail over a distance of two and a half miles north of Bear Pond on the Blue ridge, toward Chimney Rock at Harper's Ferry. The party will leave Washington early Sunday morning by automobile for Harper's Ferry and return to Washington Monday night, spending the night at Harper's Ferry. For those who have only Sunday available, return may be made to Washington by a 7:19 p.m. or 8:30 p.m. train. The hiking distance, each day, including the trail area cleared, will be approximately eight miles. Each member of the party should be equipped with a pair of gloves and a trail clearing implement, preferably an axe. Those who would like to join this expedition and have either Sunday or Monday available, are invited to communicate with M. H. Avery, who will be in charge of the expedition. Harper's Ferry Map.

Weekend, January 21 - 22, 1928
Belle Meade, Virginia

Trip with the Trail Club between Ashy Gap and Manassas Gap. Party will leave by automobile as early as possible in the afternoon of the 21st, returning Sunday evening. Bring cot and blankets. Saturday night will be spent at cottage of Dr. Elliott, near Linden. Come along if possible and help in this commendable work. You will be rewarded by some wonderful mountain views. Phone H. C. Anderson for particulars, as soon as possible.

Weekend, Sept 1 - 4, 1928
Skyland-Panorama, Virginia

A joint trip of the Wildflower Preservation Society and the Potomac Appalachian Trail Club. Take Luray bus at Ninth and C Streets, N.W., at 2:30 p.m., Saturday, September 1. Fare, $6.00 for round trip. The primary objective of the trip is to go over the newly opened trail from Skyland to Panorama, but three alternatives are offered: (1) Stop at Panorama, (2) Stop at Skyland, (3) Stop at Skyland Saturday night and Sunday; take a 4-mile hike from Skyland to Pricelands over Mary's Rock to Panorama.

Those obliged to do so may return Monday afternoon, but a scouting trip from Panorama northward towards Mt. Marshall and Linden, the section of the trail to be completed next, will be made Tuesday, returning Tuesday evening. Meals and lodging at Skyland, $5-6 per day. Saddle horse or carriage up to Skyland about $3.00. Hand baggage 75 cents per piece. Autos can drive to the foot of Stony Man Mountain only. Bus passengers Luray to foot of Stony Man extra. Over 30 very attractive 4 to 12 mile trails from Skyland available and well marked. Map of same obtainable at Skyland, costs 15 cents. Meals and lodging at Panorama $3.75 per day up. Leader: P. L. Ricker.

Weekend, October 13-14, 1928
Mt. Marshall, Virginia

Joint trip with Potomac Appalachian Trail Club for the purpose of becoming acquainted with the interesting section of the Blue Ridge between Chester Gap and Thornton Gap through which the Appalachian Trail will be constructed in the near future. Party will leave by private automobiles about 11 o'clock on Saturday the 13th and will camp Saturday night and on Sunday will climb Mt. Marshall, 3,374 feet high, and traverse a portion of the route of the trail along the crest of the ridge.

Wonderful views if weather is clear, and the autumn foliage should be in its glory. The ascent of the mountain is gradual, and the walk may be shortened for those not desiring to take the entire trip of about 12 miles. The automobile route will be along the Lee Highway through Fairfax and Warrenton, taking the road to Front Royal just beyond Gainesville. About two and a half miles beyond Flint Hill, take dirt road to left for about two miles. Leaders, P. L. Ricker and H. C. Anderson.

Weekend, November 17-18, 1928

Trail Club trip of 12 miles on Saturday from Paris to Linden, Va., and Sunday climb High Knob (2,385 ft.) southwest of Linden to scout out a route to Chester Gap on the Front Royal Road, distance about eight miles. Bus, meals, and lodging and train fare back $8.43. Leader, Mr. Schairer. (January-April 1929 schedules missing.)

Weekend, May 17-19, 1929
Panorama and Skyland, Virginia

Trail Club trip. Transportation by private auto or Luray bus leaving 9th and Pennsylvania Avenue station at 2:30 p.m. Friday. Fare $6.

Lodging and meals about $7.50. Leave Panorama 10 a.m. Saturday, hike over Mary's Rock nine miles to Skyland. Last four miles of trip may be made on horseback by making reservations ahead at cost of $6.00 round trip. Make reservations from Mr. Avery or Miss Hendershott.

Weekend, June 15-16, 1929

Mr. Avery has published an excellent description of the local sections of the Appalachian Trail, giving all points of access by auto, bus, or train and convenient lodging places if more than one-day trips are contemplated. Copies of this article may be obtain by sending a two cent stamp to H. C. Anderson, Metropolitan Bank Building, Washington, D.C.

Sunday, March 13, 1932

Joint trip with the Trail Club to Pen Mar, Pennsylvania., and Raven Rock Hollow. This is a very attractive region and an 8 or 13 mile hike may be taken. Those taking the whole of either trip will have to go by bus, leaving south side of Treasury at 7 a.m. sharp. Send reservations to C. P. Thomas, accompanied by check for $3.25 for Trail Club members and $3.75 for non-members. Any one desiring to use their own car, walking 3 or 4 miles on the trail and returning to the starting point should drive to Pen Mar, about 70 miles, and inquire way to High Rock, about 2 miles off the main road, where the hike starts. Autos need not meet at Treasury, but should reach High Rock by 9:30 a.m. Anyone desiring to go by auto or having room for passengers notify Mr. Ricker.

First Log Entries in First Cabin

Sexton Cabin Logbook
Saturday –Sunday, March 21-22, 1931

Spring is HERE—snow depth inside shelter, 2 inches; outside shelter 2 feet. Weather conditions—A rip snorting blizzard from the east swooping in like a lion from the stark slopes of Old Rag. This expedition is the official bar fastening group.

1 – Bar Examiner, [unreadable name], Danville, NY
2 – Adjuster, X (his mark)
3 – Bar Fly (from way back), Tawm Griffin (Old Rag)
4 – Bar Snooper, Myron Glaser, Old Rag, Va, and Rochester, NY
5 – Bar Rail, Johannis Franciscus Schairer
6 – Bar Tender, C. E. Tilley, Cambridge, England

Dedication of the original Sexton Cabin, 1929

Subscribed to and sworn (very profane) to me this 22nd day of March 1931—William Anderson-Brown, President, Apple Jack Exchange, Old Rag, Va.

April 18, 1931

Party consisting of S. H. Marsh, Park Supervisor, State C&D Commission; C. W. Spitler, landowner, this tract; J. W. Huffman, landowner, this tract; E. L. Price, landowner, tract adjoining on south; A. Ferdinand Zerkel, "Park Nut." Made coffee to accompany lunches carried from Valley; the purpose of this visit being consideration of Rights of Way over these tracts for the Skyline Highway.

Twenty Five Years Ago

By Kathryn Fulkerson
April 1955

I remember that many important things were happening in the Spring of 1930. The young Club was incorporated, a Membership Card was adopted, and an Emblem for the Club, a bronze button embodying the AT monogram, was distributed to the members. The Photograph Meeting and Contest, sponsored by Ridsdale Ellis, was a great success and was to become an annual event. The Sexton Shelter, the first of the long chain of shelters, was about to become a reality.

Overnight Club Trips were popular and well attended. The famous Old Rag Pilgrimage led by Myron Glaser and Tom Griffin over the February 22 holiday had an attendance of 72 persons. A cold night spent at a Sperryville hotel was followed by an exhilarating climb up Old Rag on Sunday and was made even more interesting by the Glaser-Griffin technique.

The coldest of all overnight trips, however, was at Bluemont on March 23, when even the rugs from the floor were used to supplement the inadequate bedding. Next day, the 15.5 mile hike to Harper's Ferry was full of interest: the Deer Lick, Geyser Spring, Bear Pond, and many ruins of Civil War fortifications. In contrast to the icy, cold weather at Morelands, the end of the hike nearing Harper's Ferry was spent vainly fighting a furiously raging forest fire. It was too far advanced to check, however, and had to be left to burn itself out days later.

The never-to-be-forgotten dinner at Harper's Ferry that night has gone down in club history. Jefferson Rock Hotel at the foot of the Old Historic Steps has long since vanished, but not the memory of that most plentiful of all feasts where 36 varieties of food were served at one time.

The next important trip that spring was Frank Schairer's Hazel Country Trip, April 27, which brought out some 75 hikers. The suspicious native men in this territory attempted to discourage further in-

Hikers in Hazel Hollow. On right, from left, Jack Dodson, Frank Schairer, Dodson's son, Malcolm Wood. Note measuring wheel on ground.

roads into their mountain-still country by setting fire to the under-brush on both sides of the Trail. The hikers managed to climb safely out of the Hollow and out of danger, but the incident added some excitement to the trip.

The big event of 1930 was the Fourth Annual Appalachian Trail Conference held at Skyland May 30th - June 1st, 1930, with 160 in attendance. Representatives from all the various sections of the Trail from Maine to Georgia were there. Major Welch presided in the absence of Arthur Perkins. Benton MacKaye gave an inspiring address on Vision and Reality. Mr. Pollock, Master of Skyland, outdid himself in hospitality and entertainment. Park and Forest Service officials were there to cooperate with the Conference. It was the most satisfying and inspiring meeting yet held, and promised a successful future for the Appalachian Trail.

Pre-Appalachian Trail Times:
A Visit to the Blue Ridge in 1926

Anonymous
January 1943

This is the story of an initial visit to the Blue Ridge Mountains of Virginia in 1926. It is the uncensored narrative of the impressions created by the Southern Appalachian Mountains on one who beheld them for the first time. For obvious reasons, this account should remain anonymous. It is a forgotten manuscript of sixteen years ago. While this is a short period of time in terms of years, the last decade has brought with it revolutionary, far-reaching changes in the lands which this narrative describes.

The October 1942 issue of the *Bulletin*, in its account of the very beginnings of the Potomac Appalachian Trail Club, struck a distinctly nostalgic note. It brought to the mind of the narrator here that, even prior to these activities, he had visited, as a stranger, these same lands which later became the route of the Appalachian Trail.

To enable the reader to appreciate the background of this story, the veil of mystery was just then, in 1926, being rolled back from the Appalachian regions. The Acts of Congress creating the Shenandoah and Great Smoky Mountains National Parks had just been passed. These parks were the result of a wide search of all the terrain in the East for suitable localities for inclusion in the great National Park system. There was then no Appalachian Trail technique, with its system of marked trails. Such a thing as a paint blaze had not yet been evolved. Guidebooks and literature for the Southern Appalachians were totally non-existent.

Up in New England a man by the name of Arthur Perkins was trying to revive interest in Benton MacKaye's defunct proposal, of five years earlier, to build a long trail throughout the length of the Eastern Atlantic States. Where such a trail would go in Virginia, if built, was nebulous. Would it lead near Skyland, or along the crest of the still more unknown ridges to the west?

Thus the Shenandoah region beckoned to the writer as a land which would some day come into a deserved renown. It seemed opportune to explore it.

To this venturer, the Southern Appalachians were a land of mystery. The mountaineers were a lawless lot who ran stills, defied the law and shot at strangers. Snakes would strike the unwary traveler. Altogether, it was a forbidding, inhospitable land.

Such was the background, and the knowledge gained from popular accounts, which this traveler brought from other lands. It was far from the Blue Ridge of song and story.

The narrative which follows was written as a distinctly personal account to explain in detail to those with whom he had traveled elsewhere just what impressions this new Southern Appalachian region had created.

Travel along the unmarked ridge crest was understandably slow. The distance from Thornton Gap to Skyland today may be covered on foot in a few hours over the well-marked Trail; the writer, in 1926, spent the first two days of his journey in completing the same section.

The narrative follows:

Our original intention was to walk along the crest of the Blue Ridge within the proposed Shenandoah National Park, but we diverted somewhat from this plan in order to do some east and west exploring, which gave us a better idea of the region.

We went from Washington by bus over the Lee Highway to Luray. At the height of the road in Thornton Gap we left the bus, turned south, and commenced to climb. From Thornton Gap to the top of Mary's Rock, possibly two miles, the proprietor of Panorama (a resort on the highway at Thornton Gap) has a trail. From this point to a section marked "Fields" on the map, there is no trail. We spent the first night at a spring near the head of Hughes River on the back of Pinnacle Mountain. Still following the ridge south, the next day we reached Skyland. Now came something that made our trip pleasanter and easier. Just before leaving Washington, my companion happened to see Mr. G. Freeman Pollock, the proprietor of Skyland. Mr. Pollock was much interested in our venture. People come to Skyland to ride but never to walk. We were oddities in this respect and he welcomed us. So we stayed that night in a Cabin at Skyland. The next day, we walked east to Old Rag Post Office and down the road to where White Oak Run crosses the road. This we followed up nearly to Nigger Run, where the scenic section of the Canyon begins. As it was getting dark, we retraced our steps to Old Rag Village. I had my pack, but my companion did not have his, so we sought accommodations in one of the mountain cabins in the valley. We stayed that night with Major (given name) Thornton Smith. He was a fine type of mountaineer, six feet in height and weighing over two hundred pounds. The people in this valley are all very hospitable. We stopped and talked with many of them. They are typical mountain people and regard themselves as such; but the Blue Ridge in northern Virginia is narrow and they are not so far from the valley. Also, Skyland has brought work for them, and contact with people from the outside. Smith's cabin consisted of a living room; the kitchen was an attached shed on the back. We slept in a garret amidst all sorts of drying fruits and herbs. (I had there some remarkably good wild grape preserves.)

The next morning we climbed Old Rag, a picturesque peak, and sheet rock at the top, the sort of mountain which, when you see, you inwardly resolve to climb. At the top we saw an igneous rock, different from that around it, and noticed a stone covered with inscriptions. One bore the date of 1781 and several were early 1800. We could not tell whether it was a "plant" or not but it looked aged. Mr. Pollock had never heard of the stones.

Next, we returned to White Oak Canyon. This is one of the finest, wildest, and most impressive places to have ever been. In three miles White Oak Run falls 1,500 feet. The only still water is in the pools under the falls, but it is not correct to say "falls," for it is one continuous fall all the way. There are at least six falls as fine as the one shown in the Skyland Folder. The side of the Canyon, at the bottom, must slope back nearly a thousand feet. The timber is first growth; no one could lumber in there. I never saw such white oak and tulip trees, nor finer hemlocks. The Run is a fine trout stream. We saw eight trout; it would seem almost impossible to fish the place out. We were told the mountain people had taken "tons" of trout out of that Run; they use seines. It is the finest fly casting water I would ever want. White Oak Canyon, four miles long, alone would justify the proposed Park. There is no trail through the Canyon. Scrambling from rock to rock with a thirty pound pack is hard work. We had a swim at the regulation swimming pool near the Bridge; it was cold.

I neglected to say that I found something nearly equal to the famous Katahdin scrub. It was not ordinary underbrush but "White Oak scrub." From Stony Man peak it looked like a smooth field of grain. We had come through it on the second day. It was so close that it wrenched my Hudson's bay ax from the bottom of pack, and I did not even know that it was gone. It took such an exertion to drive one's way through this growth that the extra pull was not noticeable. When I turned at the edge of the scrub, and found my ax was gone, I wanted to go back for it, but I could hardly tell where I had come out of that scrub!

That night Mr. Pollock came back to Skyland and brought with him Mr. Arno Cammerer, Assistant Director of the National Park Service, who was making an unofficial inspection of the Park area. Mr. Pollock knew the psychology of the situation. He had one of his cooks, a wonder at Southern foods, come up from the valley. On the three nights we stayed there it was camping de luxe. I had ten southern dishes which I had never eaten before. One had to walk to counteract the effect of this sort of living. Mr. Cammerer is a fine fellow and was much interested in our tramping in the proposed Park. He wanted to see all of my equipment. The Bergans Meis pack and tent so impressed him that he asked me to put it on display when his Park Superintendents come to Washington for a conference.

My companion was born in the Blue Ridge in the southwestern part of Virginia and, as he was praising the virtues of our host of the previous evening and mountain people in general, Mr. Pollock said that we had seen on that occasion one extreme and he would show us the other extreme, a condition of poverty and wretchedness which we would hardly believe could exist in these days. The section he sent us to was Broken Back Run, where lived three families. We would be the second party that had been there in five years. Once before he had taken guests there, but it had depressed them, so he had never repeated it. The first cabin had been built by a subscription raised by the guests at Skyland, for their former cabin had been so wretched. Here were living a grandfather, three sons, and a boy nineteen years old about four feet high. There were three sisters; those who were married had married their first cousins of the same name. There were from ten to twelve children, all barefoot and barely covered with ragged clothing. The beds were planks built out from the wall, covered with a mass of rags. On a steel bed which had come when the cabin was built, there was one quilt, worn through in half a dozen places, showing the rusty springs. The place was beyond description. The grandfather was not so bad, but each generation had grown worse. The old man told us how he had shot down a drunken young mountaineer, his married nephew, who had thrown rocks at his house, and left the body there for a day. The boy had shot his own father, he said, and had only gotten paid back. What details he could not remember, the sons supplied, and when their memories lapsed, the daughters, who were mixed up in the affair, volunteered.

The next place was a shack ten feet square. Here lived a man, wife, and four children. In spite of their diseased condition, these people are remarkably prolific. But next was one of the other extreme. This man had a large corn field, potatoes, cabbage, several pigs, cattle and lived a life ideal in its vigorous comfort and independence. He is a sort of king-pin among the mountain people. He even has a pool where he raises trout to sell to Skyland. This man is shrewd and able. He is the leader of the mountain moonshiners. In addition to telling us that everybody in Virginia knew him, he said he was the only man in the mountains whom they would let make moonshine, and he is not far wrong. The enforcement is under the state laws; the informer gets $100 and that is a lot of money to the mountain people. Brother tells on brother, or, as Mr. Pollock says, Ma tells on Pa and Ma goes to jail because she is the easiest spared; so as a result, little liquor is made in the mountains. While this is probably true, there seemed to be plenty of liquor in evidence and easily obtainable. One may wonder whether we had the experience sometimes heard of, that of strangers being considered as revenue officers. We did not; as far as we knew we aroused nobody's suspicions, but neither was there

Mountain Family, Shenandoah National Park, 1929

anything of which they might have been suspicious.

The next day we climbed Hawksbill and Stony Man again. Then I went with my companion to the foot of the mountain. Guests reach Skyland from Luray; from the main road which may be traversed by automobile, one follows a road along the top of a sloping ridge running out to the west for four miles into Skyland. I came back to Skyland over it that night. This day's travel totaled twenty miles.

The last day, and one on which I did not carry a pack, was the hardest. The National Parks party was headed for Rhododendron

Swamp, fifteen miles from Skyland. There was a horse available but, realizing that the trip on horseback would ruin me, I decided to walk. I left two hours early and arrived at Honeymoon Bungalow, a camp belonging to a rich farmer in the valley, at 10 o'clock. The party was to take dinner in the cabin of a mountaineer, and I carried instructions and some provisions for this meal. The family, of ten, told me that their mother was over in the potato field a mile away. Her father had walked 10 miles that day to vote, but was back and with her. The potato field was a mile from the cabin and at an altitude of 3,000 feet. It was so steep that one wondered how the potatoes stayed there. The woman and her father were digging the potatoes with a mattock, but she returned to the cabin to cook dinner. I got a mountain lad to show me the way to the top of Fork Mountain, on which there was a fire tower. That kid, undersized as he was, nearly walked my legs off me. We went up a gradual slope for 2,000 feet for three miles. At the top, I had the finest view of the whole range. To the east lay the Piedmont foothills, and to the west the Shenandoah Valley and the Massanutten Mountains which divide the Valley in half.

Near the top was a "sag" and in a clearing there I found one apple tree which was so fine that I added to my burdens two dozen apples to carry back, which indicates how good those apples were!

In one thing these mountains differ from those of New England. The soil is thick over the ledges and capable of cultivation wherever it is level. Some of the soil, although containing large boulders, is very fertile. The New England mountains have the boulders, but the glacier has scraped off the soil. I saw a cornfield which had so many boulders in it that it looked like a sea beach; yet the corn grew there.

To return to the trip: From Fork Mountain I retraced my steps to Honeymoon Bungalow where we had dinner. I walked the remaining twelve miles in two hours and three quarters. My total distance for that day, horseback trails all the way, was thirty-five miles in eight and three quarter hours. Mr. Pollock said I had the local record, but of course people never walk in that country; they ride. I told him that some time I would bring three or four friends who would make some real records for him. If I name them it will only make it tougher for some poor chap who gets beguiled into going on a stroll with them.

On Wednesday, I hiked down off the mountain and returned to Washington with Mr. Cammerer in his car.

On Tuesday's trip I saw several things of much interest. One was the Rhododendron Swamp to which I have referred. It was at the base of Fork Mountain. Rhododendron, which is rare in that section, grew for half a mile along both banks of the upper Rapidan River. Back from the strip of rhododendron on both sides grew laurel. The whole made a swamp half a mile square. Its thickness can best be told by repeating the story the mountain boy told me. He said that when hunting rabbits, if the rabbit started for the swamp, the hunter called off the dogs and made no attempt to follow the game; it was absolutely safe in the swamp. What a mass of bloom it must be in the spring!

Every clearing seemed to have an apple tree or two. In addition, we found wild grapes. Where the blight had failed to kill entirely some hardier tree, there were a few chestnuts. There were also hickory nuts and black and white walnuts. One could live for a while on that country.

Between Fishers Gap and the Honeymoon Bungalow I passed through a scene impressive in its aspect of desolation, and also a tribute to the destructive powers of the chestnut blight. This section must at one time have been entirely a pure chestnut grove. Now every tree was dead. All the trees had been uprooted and lay flat on the ground. The rains and the snow had washed away the dead bark and bleached the trunks a grayish white. No underbrush of any sort grew there. The area was as free from tree growth as are some of the western plains. These chestnuts were of tremendous size, a foot to two or three feet in diameter. Now it is a graveyard of giant trees. I have seen sections in the North where mature timber has been killed by fire but never did any compare with the utter desolation here. The area was easily two square miles. The people around this region burn nothing but dead chestnut, yet it seemed as if none had been taken away. All through the forest one sees dead chestnut trees. Selling chestnuts had been a source of income and the mountain people feel the loss of the chestnut trees most keenly.

One is always asked about snakes in the Blue Ridge. It was too cold for any to be out, but in the spring it is not a good country through which to force one's way. I did carry some potassium permanganate crystals as a measure of precaution, in spite of the season. I tried to collect all the snake stories I could. The best one was told me by Major Thornton Smith. This summer his boy was with a party that found a den on Pinnacle Mountain which contained eighty-four. Mr. Pollock told us one. He always would say that there were no snakes near Skyland, and offered a reward for a den within so many miles of Skyland. The reward was not claimed for a long time, but finally a mountain man came and wanted to show him a den. Suspicious of a plant, and understanding that rattlesnakes, if moved, will not stay in the new location. Mr. Pollock waited a few days. But it proved to be a genuine den. He captured twenty-six in all, which were presented to museums. In August, Major Thornton Smith was with a party picking huckleberries. One of the men was bitten on the finger. A string was tied around the finger, then, with a knife, a large portion of the man's finger was scraped away and the wound sucked. My mountain boy told me of other non-fatal cases. The one fatal case of which I heard was where a man unused to liquor was bitten and made to drink a quart of whiskey. The doctor said that the liquor finished him. The snake venom does depress heart action. It is at this stage, not at the time of the initial bite, that a stimulant might be useful.

The foliage was remarkable. Trees not native to New England impart colors which the northern woods do not have. I had thought the New England woods beyond comparison, but I must admit the superior coloring in this region. Late October and November are the ideal times to tramp in the Blue Ridge.

Camping technique at this time was a totally unknown science. The trip described here was made in the very beginning of the development of lightweight camping technique. The enthusiastic comments on matters which are today commonplace may seem naive. They do, however, better reflect pre-Trail conditions.

Now as to equipment. We planned to provide for ourselves for ten days. I carried thirty-five pounds. I had a Bergans Meis pack, and how comfortably it carried! However, it did seem to pull away from my back where the semicircular piece of leather appears on the frame. No alteration of straps seemed to change this condition. I had a pair of Bean hiking shoes, rain shirt, and pants. Because of mud, on every day except the last (that of my thirty-five mile hike) I wore a pair of Army trench boots. I knocked out every hob nail on the trip. I am through with these soft iron hobs used by shoemakers. In the future I intend to try the hobs sold by Bean, or some of the sharp, pointed English nails. I spent one entire day in the rain and was much pleased with the way I could travel in the rain shirt and trousers; I even used them to sleep in. For a tent, I had the Von Lengerke and Detmold one man tent, plenty of room for two, which is vermin, mosquito, and snake proof. Of course, these features were not needed, but it weighs only six pounds and I consider it the finest lightweight tent I have seen.

As to food: Bread was made in a fry pan, by using prepared self-rising flour which requires the addition only of water. We carried sliced bacon. For breakfast we made fine cakes with self-rising buckwheat flour, by adding egg powder and Klim, in liquid form. I was experimenting with other foods I got from Von Lengerke and Detmold. They proved an unqualified success and the solution of the food problem on a long trip. Egg powder is supposed to be good for omelets and scrambled eggs, but one would have to be very hungry to eat the stuff; it is almost nauseating. For tea, I used Tabloid tea; two hundred cups to a can two inches long. Instant coffee does not require any boiling. For sugar we had a small tube of saccharine tablets known as Saxin. Klim you are familiar with. The soups were extremely nutritious; they cook up into a heavy soup which is very sustaining. The soup tubes were 3" x 1" and come in all flavors. To these we sometimes added dehydrated vegetables. Of the latter we had potatoes, turnips, spinach, and cranberries; with the last we even succeeded in making a jelly. These vegetables take over a half hour to cook but they are excellent substitutes for the green articles. When one considers their weight, an ounce for eight portions, their value is apparent.

Some Early AT History

by Benton MacKaye
January 1953

At the unveiling May 6, 1957, of Joe Winn's master mural of Old Rag Mountain at PATC Headquarters in Washington, I made a few remarks concerning the early story of the AT. Since then, Joe and his Joan have asked me to extend said remarks for the record, telling how I came to "conceive" and "name" the Appalachian Trail. So here goes.

It goes back some sixty years. The first notion of a long-distance footway started forming while with the man who gave me my first look into a real wilderness. He was James Sturgis Pray, afterward head of landscape architecture at Harvard University. With him and a couple of other primeval souls, Draper Maury and Robert Mitchell, I spent several weeks in the White Mountains of New Hampshire in the summer of 1897.

A few years later, in 1903, I joined Sturgis when he, as an official of the AMC (Appalachian Mountain Club), was laying out what I think was the first long-distance footpath up to date. It was long for then, but not for now. It went east and west connecting two sets of local short-distance paths: An eastern set of paths in the Passaconaway Chocorua Range and a western set of paths in the Franconia Range.

Before this, in the summer of 1900, I had made an expedition with another pioneer in the reverse art of leading civilization to the wilderness. He was Horace Hildreth, a fellow student at Harvard. We did the Green Mountains of Vermont from Haystack Mountain via Killington Peak to Mt. Mansfield. By back road, cart path, and sheer bushwhacking, we went Vermont's Long Trail 10 years before it was born.

During these 10 years (1900-10), I got acquainted with Allen Chamberlain of Boston. Like Sturgis, he stood high in AMC's councils. By pen as well as hoof he was a pathfinder. He wrote what was, I think, the first dissertation on long-distance footways: a paper for the Society of American Foresters. I had the honor of reading it at a meeting of that Society in Gifford Pinchot's home here in Washington (about 1912). It was during these experiences (between 1897 and 1912), that my own notions of a north-south mountain footway must have been conceived; but another decade passed before they developed and were named the "Appalachian Trail" (1921).

I spent some of the summer of 1921 with my friend Charles Harris Whitaker at his home in the highlands of New Jersey. I talked with him about the trail idea, and he liked it.

"But what to do about it, Charlie?"

"Well," he said, "you write it up, and I'll print it as an article in the *Journal*."

"Next," said Charlie, "I'll introduce you to a man named Clarence Stein, the chairman of the Institute's Committee on Community Planning. He's just the man to help get it going."

Accordingly, there appears this note in my diary:

> *Sunday, July 10, 1921. Spent the day with Charlie at Hudson Guild Farm (near Netcong, N. J.)....*
>
> *P.M., talk with Clarence Stein and C. about Appal. trail project.*

Result: the *Journal of the American Institute of Architects* published my proposal, to wit: "An Appalachian Trail: A Project in Regional Planning." Specifically, a footpath "over the full length of the Appalachian skyline, from the highest point in the north to the highest point in the south, from Mt. Washington to Mt. Mitchell." This article came out in October. Reprints were made. They came to me in Shirley Center, Mass., says my diary, on November 8.

The first gun was fired by Clarence S. Stein, in his Introduction on the reprint, as follows:

> *The big cities of America seem to have been planned and developed as working places...Parks are generally afterthoughts...As the cities expand they devour the surrounding forests and farms... The only relief from the noise and*

strain of the industrial community is the quiet of unmolested nature...We need the big sweep of bills or sea as tonic for our jaded nerves. And so Mr. Benton MacKaye offers us a new theme in regional planning...

He would as far as is practicable conserve the whole stretch of the Appalachian Mountains for recreation. Recreation in the biggest sense, the re-creation of the spirit that is being crushed by the machinery of the modern industrial city...

The great Appalachian Trail is already started. The Appalachian Mountain Club, the Green Mountain Club, and other similar organizations have for years past been laying the foundation for just such a scheme as is here outlined...[So] the elements needed...are already in existence, but to organize the systematic development of the vast recreational plan presented in this article will necessitate the cooperation of many minds and many talents. For the purpose of securing constructive criticism the Committee on Community Planning (AIA) is sending out a limited number of copies of this article.

The early germination of the scheme we can now follow sketchily via sundry notations from my diaries.

Nov. 9, Shirley Center: P. M., planning distrib. Appal. reprints.

Nov. 26, Boston: Lunch with Allen Chamberlain, good talk with A. on trail.

Dec. 9, Boston: P.M., attended N. Engl. Trail Conf., met Comey and Turner. Good meeting.

Arthur C. Comey, landscape architect, Cambridge, was Secretary of this New England Trail Conference (NETC). Albert M. Turner, field secretary, Connecticut Forest and Park Commission, Hartford, was elected NETC chairman for the next year.

Dec. 10 (Conference continued): A.M.at N. Engl. Trail Conf.,

Comey referred to my work (AT article). Lunch with Kelsey, Nolan,
Allen (Chamberlain) et al.

Harlan P. ("Kel"), Kelsey, landscape architect and nurseryman, was then and since has been a very active leader in conservation movements. In 1920's he served with Maj. Wm. A. Welch and others on the commission appointed to locate the two prospective eastern national parks, Shenandoah and Great Smoky Mountains. John Nolan, Sr., was the first man, to my knowledge, who was known as a member of the then new profession of city planning.

March 16, Boston: Lunch with Allen Chamberlain & talk
on Appal. Project, same with P. W. Ayres. Saw H. N. Shepard.

Philip W. Ayres, forester for The Society for the Protection of New Hampshire Forests, was, with Allen Chamberlain and Harvey N. Shepard, one of the prime movers in getting the White Mountains National Forest, via passage of the Weeks law in 1911, established.

March 18, Hartford: Lunch with Albert M. Turner & Austin
Hawes & talk on trail, 2-5:30. Great business. Austin F.
Hawes, state forester of Connecticut, was and since has been
a national figure in forestry.
March 21, New York: Lunch with Clarence Stein & Torrey
at City Club, long talk (on AT).

Raymond H. Torrey, journalist, botanist and conservation leader, was the prime mover in developing woodland trails in the region between the Hudson and the Delaware, especially in the highlands of Bear Mountain Interstate Park. He wrote a weekly nature column in the *New York Evening Post* entitled "Long Brown Path." He wrote the first broadside news story of the Appalachian Trail, outlining' the whole project (*New York Evening Post*, April 7, 1922). From this time until his death in 1938 Torrey proved to be an institution in himself toward advancing the AT across the Hudson-Delaware section.

March 25: Saw Daniel C. Beard, Nat'l Scout Comm'r, at Flushing, gave me names &c.

Daniel C. Beard was the highest uniformed officer of the Boy Scouts of America.

April 6: Eve, supper, eve at City C. with CSS, Torrey, Welch, Allis et al., planning NY-NJ Conf.

Maj. Wm. A. Welch, then director of the Bear Mountain Interstate Park was a conservation leader of nationwide reputation. He took an immediate interest in. the AT; and in 1925 became the first chairman of the AT Conference. He devised the AT monogram (the crossbar of the A coinciding with that of the T). J. Ashton Allis was a leader and corraller of the region's outdoor clubs.

It was at this April 6 session at the City Club in New York that Torrey definitely proposed "what you might call a New York-New Jersey Trail Conference. This NYNJTC became for the Mid-Atlantic domain what NETC was already for the North Atlantic.

April 12, W a s h i n g t o n: Lunch with Schmeckebier, with him to Matthes, Geol. S.

L. F. Schmeckebier, economist, Brookings Institute, and Francois E. Matthes, geologist, USGS, both were leaders in the outdoor world. They were the first men contacted by me for aid toward the AT in the Washington area. They were suggested to me by Allen Chamberlain.

April 13: (Evening) Meeting at Penguin Club, formation of Appalachian Trail Com. of Wash. to further Appal. Trail.

About a dozen were present. Of these, F. E. Matthes was made chairman of the said committee, and L. F. Schmeckebier, secretary. Among the others were: Frederick M. Kerby, journalist and conservation leader, on the then Scripps-McRay newspaper chain. Harry A. Slattery, secretary of the recently formed National Conservation Association; subsequently became Assistant Secretary of the Interior. Mr. and Mrs. Louis F. Post. Mr. Post was formerly the editor of the Chicago *Public*, as well as former Assistant Secretary of Labor under President Wilson. Two men, both foresters in the U. S. Forest Service, were later added to the committee: Franklin W. Reed and Raphael Zon.

> *April 19: P. M., saw Cammerer of Nat'l Parks Serv.*

Arno C. Cammerer, then Director of National Park Service, took keen interest from the start in the AT project. Through him the initial plans were made for the Shenandoah and Great Smoky Mountains National Parks, including provisions for routing through them the Appalachian Trail.

> *April 23 (Sunday) : All day trip to Harpers Ferry (lunch there), Berryville, Snickers Gap, and return. Two autos, Fred's with family (Fred Kerby) & Slat, Rosalie with self, Reid, Matthes, & Dr. Brown.*
>
> *Eve, at Fred's, glorious day.*
>
> *"Slat" refers to Harry Slattery; Rosalie, to Miss Rosalie Jones, former woman suffragist leader.*
>
> *April 25, New York: Supper at City Club with CSS, Torrey, Allis, et al.*
>
> *Eve. adjourned to "Log Cabin"--meeting of about 30 formed the "NY-NJ Trail Conf."*

Thus Torrey's proposal, made about 3 weeks previously, now took definite shape, and the federation of the region's outdoor clubs was formally established. This little institution, under Torrey's effective leadership, was to do yeoman service in advancing the AT from the Connecticut line to the Delaware Water Gap.

> *May 2: P. M. writing letters [to] Dr. Hedges et al.*

Dr. H. S. Hedges, of Charlottesville, Va., took a vigorously active interest in the AT. He made a special trip to scout a route along the Blue Ridge adjacent to his home and sent me a valuable report thereon. (See files of the PATC.)

> *June 10 A. M. . . . began notes on Constitution of "The Appal. Trail, Inc."*

This was the first draft of the constitution adopted 3 years later (1925), when the first AT Conference was organized at the Hotel Raleigh, in Washington. Besides the persons mentioned in these daily notes, I contacted in person or by letter during this spring of 1922 several important officials. Clinton Smith and Verne Rhodes, of the U. S. Forest Service, took measures to have the AT routed through the southern national forests (Virginia, North Carolina, and Georgia). Paul M. Fink, of Jonesville, Tenn., took the initiative in AT development in the Virginia-Tennessee section.

> *Nov. 24, Shirley Center: P. M., went to village, met Clarence S. at 1:00 train. Cram brought us up. Lunch, talked, walked, all three of us, Thacher Road. (Third member was my brother James.)*
>
> *Eve, went over "agenda" with CSS.*
>
> *Nov. 25: A. M., Walk with CSS to store. Talk with him at home on plans for Appal. project. Walk with him to Benjamin Hill.*
>
> *Nov. 26: A. M., Long breakfast & talk with CSS & James on project. Saw CSS off on 10.56 to Boston & N. Y. Walked home. Sawed wood.*

These three November days of 1922 comprised what Clarence (CSS) has ever since cheerfully recalled as "The Shirley Conference." We reviewed the work of our first year, October 1921 to November 1922. Good starts had been made in at least four sections: (1) New England via the NETC. (2) Hudson-Delaware via the NYNJTC. (3) Virginia, through the work of Dr. H. S. Hedges of Charlottesville. (4) Southern section via the U. S. Forest Service (Smith, Rhodes, and

Zon), and the work of Paul M. Fink of Jonesboro.

Next we laid out steps to fill the gaps. My brother James was a helpful adviser in all this.

1923

The new year started well via the 2-day annual meeting of the New England Trail Conference at AMC Headquarters, 5 Joy Street, Boston, Friday and Saturday, January 19 and 20. Following are notations thereof from my diary:

> *Jan. 19: P. M., NETC meeting, Sturgis Pray spoke, met all the crowd.*
> *Eve, NETC dinner & meeting con'd.*
> *Jan. 20: A. M.--NETC meeting. Gave talk (on AT project).*
> *Resolution of approval passed.*

This 2-day meeting of the NETC was basic in clinching the start we had made (CSS and self) in advancing the AT from the White Mountains of New Hampshire to Massachusetts and Connecticut. The meetings were chaired by Bert Turner, of Forest and Park Commission of Hartford. Incidentally, he had just "batched it" with me on Christmas Day at my home in Shirley Center. Sturgis Pray, my old camp teacher, also took a prominent part. These men, with Allen Chamberlain, proved powerful pillars in the foundation structure of the Appalachian Trail both in New England and through its entire length.

From New England we now move to the Hudson. Again my diary:

> *Oct. 26, Bear Mtn. Inn, Palisades Interstate Park, on the Hudson: P. M., Took auto ride to Storm King. Drove with Bill Howard, A. C., Kelsey, Lewis M.*
> *Eve, Held App. T. Conf. (See memo.)*
> *Bear Mtn. Conference, Bear Mtn. Inn.*

I gave talk on idea of the Appal'n project, followed by discussion of possibilities of linking trail feature with forest fire protection. Wilbur of N.J. and Bill Howard of N.Y. took main part (with self). Then talked trail progress. Allen Chamberlain told of poss's of Mass. officially extending Appal'n Trail thru Berkshires. Meeting 8:30-10:45.

Among the people present at this gathering, besides the ones already introduced to the reader, there were:

Miss Harlean James, Washington, D.C., secretary of the American Planning and Civic Association.

Miss Gertrude Stein, New York, sister of Clarence, leader of outdoor activity at Hudson Guild Farm.

Wm. G. Howard, Albany, chief forester, State of New York.

C. A. Hartnagle, Albany, assistant state geologist, New York.

C. P. Wilbur, Trenton, state forester, New Jersey.

Lewis Mumford, New York, author of books on architecture, cities, and the then budding doctrine of regionalism.

Oct. 27: A. M., Took walk with crowd over Bear Mtn.

P.M., Took bus with crew to Beach Bottom. Torrey took them on AT over Black Mtn.

Eve, Second meeting, discussed Trail sections, geol. & hist. features.

Oct. 28: A. M., Trip up Anthony's Nose, 14 on trip, Torrey et al.

P. M., Lunch with Kelsey, CSS & Torrey. Meeting of conf., decided to adopt AT design (the Welch Monogram).

Getting ready, to cabin with CSS. All took 5:41 train to N.Y.

Eve (New York), supper with Kelsey, City Club, & talk.

This 3-day Bear Mountain meeting did for the Hudson-Delaware section what the January NETC meeting of 1923 did for the New England section, clinching work already done, crystallizing plans for next steps.

1925

March 1 (Sun.) Washington: A. M. wrote "constitution" for AT Conf. & suggested plan for actual work.
March 2: A. M., Met CSS at Raleigh--lunch with him.
Meeting 3 P. M, Maj. Welch presided. Opening welcome by Mr. Delano, Pres., The Federated Societies. I spoke on the AT project, followed CSS, Torrey, F. F. Schentz, Frank Place.
Eve, dinner at Raleigh & meeting, speakers: Comey on "going light"; Adolph on "forest fire service"; Matthes on "nature guide service."
March 3: AT Conf.
A. M., Talks by Rupp of Pa., Pollock of Va., Hedges of Va., Fink of Tenn., Cooper of Vt., Brown of Md., Clinton Smith, and Miss Harlean James.
Luncheon. Mather spoke. Stephen Mather, first Director or Nat'l Parks Serv.
P. M., Business meeting. Made Conf. permanent, elected Executive Committee of fifteen (Welch Chairman).

This 2-day Hotel Raleigh Conference of 1925, inaugurated the overall federation of local outing clubs, northern and southern, which has grown to the present virile outdoor institution carrying on from Katahdin to Oglethorpe under its illustrious banner, "Appalachian Trail Conference."

1927

New England Trail Conference Jan. 21-22, AMC, 5 Joy St. Boston.

Jan. 21: P. M. session. Discussed trail facilities & reports from constituate organizations. Met Allen C., Elmer Fletcher, Torrey, Turner, Mr. Annett of Jaffrey (N.H.), Judge Perkins of Hartford, Miss Marian Buck.
Eve. session. I gave talk on "Outdoor Culture, the Phi-

losophy of Through Trails." Given splendid attention.

Next speakers, Walter O'Kane of Vt. on what we really were trying to do - education vs. boosting. Miss Buck on work on Wapack Range, lively discussion; Irving Appleby on his walk over the Vt. "Long Trail," great adventures. Bully conversations in between.

Jan. 22 (Saturday morning) : Reports from Conn. (Judge Perkins) and from R. I. on through-trails. Sprague spoke on Wachusett-Watatic Trail. Harland Sisk on trail tools.

This 2-day Boston session of NETC marked another pivotal milestone of the AT's first decade. From it emerged Judge Arthur Perkins. Major Welch, head of the AT cohorts, now desired to retire. Judge Perkins also wanted to retire from his professional career. Result, Judge Perkins replaced Major Welch as head of the AT Conference.

1928-1929

Spending the winter of 1928 29 in Hartford working under Austin F. Hawes, state forester, I saw a great deal of Judge Perkins at his home, when he was not on AT scouting trips between Katahdin and the Potomac. On two of these expeditions I joined him. Again, to my diary:

Jan, 12 (Sat.), 1929 : Annual Meeting of GMC (Green Mtn. Club), Hotel Brewick Rutland, Vt.

Breakfast with Messrs. J. Ashton Allis (N.Y.), Robert Ross (Vt. State Forester), Fred Tucker (father of Herman) & Arthur Tucker. Met Mr. Mortimer Procter and Willis Ross Pres. & Sec'y, GMC respectively.

A.M. meeting: reports of committees.

Lunch all together around long table, about 30 (30-40 in meetings).

P.M., reports front "sections", Bennington, Killington, &c.

> *Read my speech on "Why the AT?"' Judge Perkins gave talk on AT.*

Appalachian Trail Conference. Annual Meeting. May 10-11. Brainerd Hall, Lafayette College, Easton, Pa. Host, Blue Mtn. Club, Professor Eugene C. Bingham, President.

> *May 10 (Fri.), 1929: Evening. First session of AT Ann. Meeting. Judge Perkins presiding. Welcome by President W. M. Lewis of Lafayette College. I spoke on "The Origin & Conception of the AT" M. H. Avery on AT work on Va. section. Dr. H. F. Rentschler on Eastern Penna. sec.*
>
> *About 60 present. Met several men, Ex-mayor Wm. F. Shannaman (who called my speech "Emersonian"), Dr. H. F. Rentschler, and "Dan" Hoch (all pillars of the Penna. section). Among others present , Torrey, Frank Place, Turner, Hawes, Wilbur of N. J. (State Forester), Murray Stevens of N. Y., E. M. Zimmerman of Bethlehem, Pa.*
>
> *May 11 (Sat.) : A.M., Business meeting, 22 present. Lunch all together.*
>
> *P. M., Trip to Del. Water Gap. Abt. 30.*
>
> *Eve. meeting, Torrey and John Finlay Spoke.*

Among the persons named at this Easton meeting were two future AT Conference chairmen, Myron Avery and Murray Stevens. Present also at this meeting were three other persons taking initial parts in advancing the AT, H. C. ("Andy") Anderson, Marian Lapp, and Kathryn Fulkerson. They were charter members of the now celebrated Potomac Appalachian Trail Club (PATC). This institution had been started in Washington 2 years earlier (1927), happily coinciding with the inauguration of "J.P." (Judge Perkins) as head of the AT Conference.

The "big five" PATC founders were Myron Avery, "Andy," Frank Schairer, Lawrence Schmeckebier, and P. L. Ricker. The Potomac Appalachian Trail Club initiated a string of other AT clubs, notable among them being the Georgia Appalachian Trail Club. (GATC)

Myron Avery blazing the Trail, 1940

1931

This year marked my first contact with the illustrious Smoky Mountains Hiking Club (SMHC), headquarters, Knoxville, Tenn. This club was host to the AT Conference Annual Meeting held in June at Gatlinburg, Tenn., adjacent to the newly born Great Smoky Mountains National Park. This occasion called for an entertainment committee, among whose duties was that of inviting speakers to address the pantheistic multitude. The chairman of this committee was Harvey Broome, who sent me an invitation to give a talk. I sent back regrets with a statement entitled "Our 10th Birthday," which Harvey read to the festive company.

This year (1931, our 10th birthday) marked the firm establishment of the Appalachian Trail, name and all. The true and final naming consisted in placing the familiar AT monogram on strategic spots to guide robust walkers from Katahdin to Oglethorpe; namely, in blazing the trail from Maine to Georgia. Except for a few gaps, this job had been accomplished during the first decade.

Blazing the trail was accomplished by a lusty host of outdoors men and women under the stanch and magnetic leadership of three men, Major Welch, Judge Perkins, and Captain Avery, three successive chairmen of the Appalachian Trail Conference, all now having joined the immortality of timelessness.

As a concept and institution, the AT came to pass as the child of two sets of parents, even as did that other institution known as the U.S. Several states created the U. S. and the U. S. created several states; several clubs created the AT, and the AT created several clubs. The original local clubs of the northern section New Hampshire to Pennsylvania, plus the SMHC, and two United States agencies in the southern section formed the federation of the AT Conference. Inspired thereby, the AT clubs were born. The first, as already noted, was the Potomac (1927). This club, indeed, was pivotal in clinching the entire structure; it arched the gap between North and South by volunteering to take over the 500 miles of route bisected at Harpers Ferry.

And so with the coming of October in 1931, we could call it a decade on the Appalachian Trail, and say it was finished if not completed, yet or ever. At this time I wrote a sequel to my first AT document, published 10 years before. It attempted to answer the question so often put to me by J. P. (Judge Perkins) : "When we get the Trail, Ben, what are we going to do with it?"

The title of my answer was "The Appalachian Trail: Guide to the Study of Nature." It was published in the *Scientific Monthly*, vol. XXXIV, pp. 330-342. It came out 6 months after the AT's 10th birthday, in April 1932.

The best way to become acquainted with any scenery is to engage in some pursuit in it which harmonizes with it. Thoreau.

With this sentence as the text, the article began: That is why the Appalachian Trail was started, to become "acquainted with" scenery; to absorb the landscape and its influence as revealed in the earth and primeval life. The way to attain this is to do something, not just admire something; to engage in some harmonizing "pursuit;" to build a foot trail several hundred miles long through the scenery of the Appalachians on the crestline from Maine to Georgia. This is the first pursuit which several hundred young persons have accomplished during the past 10 years. Such is their first long step in the longer pursuit of becoming harmonized with scenery, and the primeval influence.

The scope of the argument may next be sensed from its few headings, to wit:

The Appalachian Trail
The Appalachian Range
Genesis of the Range
Genesis of the Forest
The Appalachian Forest
To Read the Primeval

The answer to J. P.'s question boils down to the word "pursuit." Here is the parting shot: To learn to read, first hand, on the horizon and along the stream, the big outlines of the primeval drama; to take specifically the Appalachian country as the common school and playground; to weave together the threads containing the total story of this country, even as already we have woven the separate sections of our total footpath, this appears to be the logical second stage for the second decade of our enterprise. A "pursuit" such as this, to become acquainted with our scenery, should be the next step in developing the Appalachian Trail.

Now, a quarter of a century later, another question is asked: What about the future of the Appalachian Trail? This question is admirably analyzed in the current issue of the *PATC Bulletin* (April-June 1957), by Philip J. Stone (pp. 45-46). Every AT walker, worker, and thinker should read and absorb his challenging questions. He poses about twelve of them, but they boil down to one, how to defend the remnant Appalachian wilderness against the metropolitan invasion. The answer may go to twelve times twelve, but again they come to one, to spark the will to defend our basic land. One basic method is pursuit, if not of happiness itself, then of the mystery whereof it is part: the unraveling of the greatest detective story on earth: Dame Nature's.

Interview With Benton MacKaye

by Dorothy M. Martin

"I never thought it would come to this!" exclaimed Benton MacKaye, the man who conceived the Appalachian Trail and who in 1930 received from Harold Allen the title of its "Nestor" (an old man noted for wisdom). He had completed a tour of the headquarters of the Potomac Appalachian Trail Club and was referring to the setup and the spirit of the office at 1916 Sunderland Place. I had conducted him on this his first visit at the Club since it had acquired a home of its own.

"A home indeed" it was, according to our guest, with many folks busy on a great adventure. There was Bob Hendricks working on a shelter report; there was Chris Scoredos checking dinner reservations; and Anne Simplicio typing manuscript for the *Bulletin*; Vivian Lamm and Ben Griffith holding down headquarters and shelter desks; and finally Earl Haskell and Charlie Thomas taking care of visitors.

Charlie did the honors, as only Charlie could. Starting with a raftershaking handshake and hello, he led the Nestor into every niche and corner of the place. First the maps on the wall, the profile of the range, the equipment closet and the library, possible beginnings of an all-Appalachian literary storehouse. Then downstairs to see the blankets, axes, and all the other absolute essentials for living in the open, described by Benton MacKaye as "Booted and spurred and ready to ride." Especially was he impressed with the maps and the profile which he called "the seed of a whole school of Appalachian geography."

"No, I never dreamed of the likes of this, when five and twenty years ago, I received H. C. Anderson's letter asking what did I think of the name 'Potomac' for an AT Club embracing this particular cross-section of the range."

A few nights after this, the Nestor made a short talk before our twenty-fifth birthday party, reviewing some of the early history of the project. I asked him to repeat for the record some of his salient points. " Yes," he replied, "it will give me a chance to say some of the things that I forgot, due to the unexpected and overwhelming welcome given me by that rising and magnificent audience."

So he began. "As I tried to say that night, I consider that the birth of the PATC marked the birth also of the Appalachian Trail. The formal conception came six years earlier, provided the AT Conference was correct in its wording of the artistic plaque which they generously sent me in 1948 through Bob Howes, then President of the Smoky Mountain Hiking Club. This plaque consisted of the familiar AT monogram (the invention of Major William A. Welch), a sketch map of the AT, and the words 'To Benton MacKaye, who in 1921 conceived and named the Appalachian Trail.' To my mind, the plaque itself could not have been better conceived and worded. So far as the printed record goes in the Journal of the American Institute of Architects, October 1921, I appear to have conceived the conception that a footway the length of the Appalachian Range would be something worthwhile having.

"This, however, was only the first chapter of a long story which, through the sentiment and sweat of a number of known and some forgotten souls, came to constitute the full conception brought to birth by the PATC in the good year '27. It took a few years more for the project to come of age; and while the '30's were still young, your Potomac Club, with the others from Maine to Georgia, all under the inspiring leadership of the valiant Myron Avery, placed the Appalachian Trail upon the map."

Benton MacKaye had at the dinner told something of this six-year conception period, naming a number of those "known and some forgotten souls." I asked him to repeat part of it and add anything else which came to mind. "All right," he said, I'll go back to my conception, not of the Appalachian Trail, but before that to my first notions of what constitutes a true wilderness path. These occurred long before 1921. It was in the summer of 1897 that a certain 'Moses in reverse' led me *into* the wilderness. His name was James Sturgis Pray, who later became head of Landscape Architecture at Harvard. We tramped for several weeks in the White Mountains of New Hampshire, which covered what was then a largely unmarked forest fastness. We lived in the spirit of Byron's couplet:

There is a pleasure in the pathless wood,
There is a rapture on the lonely shore.

"We experienced both in the first two days; and it must have been with these lines ringing in my ears, and up against the merciless rapture of a nigh-impassable blowdown, that the notion sprouted in me of a *path through a pathless wood*. I've been wrestling with this paradox now for five and fifty years. How to have a path, a line of accessibility, and also have a "wood," a wilderness minus the marring marks of man? Sturgis showed me how.

"Sturgis, as Councillor of Improvements of the American Moutain Club, was a pioneer in keeping improvements *out* of the wilderness. In 1903, I accompanied him while he was laying out the first through trail in the White Mountain area. It connected the East and the West, the Swift River country with the Waterville country, separated by the quite real wilderness of Carragain Notch. The path proved a great success. The Carragain wilderness was made accessible; it could now be crossed by any ordinary amateur woodsman, even a fat one, and without fear of getting lost. Though not a path-less way through the wood, it was an improvementless way which was opened by the Councillor of Improvements.

"This has always been my conception of an-honest-to-God wilderness trail. A wilderness trail presupposes a wilderness; a Carragain Trail presumes a Carragain Wilderness, and an Appalachian Trail an Appalachian Wilderness. This we have at least in spots; and where we have, my conception and Pray's coincide."

When asked about those "forgotten men" who figured in the later period from 1921 to 1927, he replied, "That marked a turning period in my life. For me it was a time of making new and enduring friendships, Gifts of God and the Appalachian Trail. Among them were two men who were quite as responsible as myself for this project. Some such pathway might have been proposed and carried out under entirely different auspices because times were ripe for a larger recognition of the wilderness influence as such, and of its rightful place alongside the urban and rural influences in the life and landscape of the country. But the Appalachian Trail, conceived as I have described it to you, would never have been save for Charles Harris Whitaker and Clarence S. Stein.

"Whitaker was the Editor of the *Journal of the American Institute of Architects*. I told him about my idea, and he suggested that I write it up for the *Journal*. This I did. Meanwhile, he introduced me to Clarence Stein, who, as the Chairman of an important A.I.A. committee, sponsored the project. My article was published in October (1921): *An Appalachian Trail: A Project in Regional Planning.*

"The Stein Committee sent out a large number of reprints, and received many enthusiastic responses. The following winter (1921-22), I looked up a number of pivotal people with whom I had personal confabs. In Cambridge, I saw my old woods teacher, Sturgis Pray, who called the project 'monumental.' Also, another old comrade, Allen Chamberlain, a former A.M.C. President, with whom I had worked back in 1908, toward establishing the White Mountain National Forest. Allen was wholeheartedly for the AT scheme, and told me to talk about it with Laurence Schmeckebier and Francois Matthes, whenever I went to Washington.

"I went to New York first, where I spent some weeks with Clarence Stein. He and I, with Charlie Whitaker and various others, used to sit in the City Club on West 44th Street and plan whom next to tackle. We discovered a prize in Raymond Torrey, who ran a weekly nature column in the New York *Evening Post*. Through him we got next to Major William A. Welch, then Director of the Bear Mountain Park, on the Hudson. I recall the evening when he, Torrey, Stein and myself sat together after dinner in the City Club, while Torrey outlined his plan to form a N.Y.-N.J. Trail Conference, designed to advance the AT across these two States. This the New England Trail Conference was later to do in its region, led by its Chairman, Albert M. Turner (incidentally, one of the big calibered, little recalled, creative minds of the country's recreational development). Torrey, about the same time, wrote for the *Evening Post* the first big broadside daily newspaper account of the entire AT project. Torrey and Turner became the rousing Rajahs of the Trail in their respective bailiwicks.

"Toward the spring of '22, I went to Washington. There I immediately got hold of 'Schmeck' and Matthes. Also, being an old Forest

Service man, I looked up some of the boys in that Bureau. My oldest friend there, Raphael Zon, gave me quiet encouragement, and suggested whom to see. There were then no eastern National Parks, and we needed the support of the southern National Forests. This we obtained through Clinton Smith, who was in charge of these far-southern domains. Also I was put in communication with one promising local official, Verne Rhodes, Supervisor of one of the southernmost Forests. Trails already followed the main ranges through all these Federal areas. 'Yes, certainly,' they would gladly consent to be links in the backbone footpath.

"But there were gaps between the Forests, with the land all in private hands. Local clubs, unlike in the north, were few and far between. However, there were at least two voices in this private wilderness that would be raised in our behalf. One was Paul Fink in East Tennessee. The other was Dr. H. S. Hedges of Charlottesville, Va. The Doctor immediately got busy exploring the Range adjacent to his home. Before this section became the Shenandoah National Park, he wrote us a voluminous report on its trail prospects, which must now repose somewhere in the files of the AT Conference.

"Came 1924. I sat with Harlan Kelsey in the old Cosmos Club. He and Major Welch were on a commission to find a pair of eastern National Parks and they found the Shenandoah and the Great Smoky Mountain playgrounds. Kelsey, sitting on a big club sofa, ordained to put the AT through the Smokies, and it was so.

"Came 1925. The first AT Conference was held in March in the Raleigh Hotel, Washington. The Major presided. One vigorous still going and not-forgotten lady was on hand, Miss Harlean James. I recall also her gallant crew, including Ruby Anderson and Mary Jo. Clarence Stein was there, and Pollock of Skyland. Andy was there, but I don't recall meeting him. 'Maine to Georgia' was laid out in six sections, and the first formal organization got launched.

"Came 1927. Two 'institutions' appeared on the AT - a Judge and a Club. Judge Arthur Perkins (the beloved 'JP') relieved the Major as chairman of the ATC. The Judge lived in Hartford, where I spent the winter of 1928-29. I sat with the Judge many an evening in his attractive home, discussing the fate of the Trail, section by section.

"We roamed the Range together, drove through the Berkshires and along the Housatonic River. We attended a resplendent three-day midwinter confab of the Green Mountain Club in Rutland. We went to Easton, Pa. to a joint gathering of the PATC and the Eagle Mountain Climbing Club, which was for me a kingpin occasion. There it was that I first laid eyes on Andy, Kathryn Fulkerson, Marian Lapp and Murray Stevens. There, too, I first met those three grand musketeers 'the Mayor' (Shannaman), 'the Doc' (Rentschler), and 'dear old Dan' (Hoch), who in Congress or out still rolls on in his middle '80's.

"So much for the pre-natal period of the Appalachian Trail, and for the illustrious souls, forgotten or not, who took their fine parts in the incubation that laid the base for the PATC. This pre-natal period was also an ice-breaking period, and most people still asked what was the big idea of having a rough improve-less way from Maine to Georgia when so many smooth improved ways already were at hand? It took a Major and a Judge to open a hole in this stiff-collared line, through which to let a Captain carry the ball to its goal."

Benton MacKaye took a long breath. As interviewer, I waited a minute before I asked him if he had any new ideas about making the most of the Trail now that it was complete? He smiled reminiscently. "That is the very question that the Judge asked me in Hartford, in 1929. By 1931, just ten years after proposing the Trail, I had a second article ready, answering the Judge's question. This appeared the following April (1932) in the *Scientific Monthly*, entitield *The Appalachian Trail: A Guide to the Study Of Nature.* "Let me read the last words in each of my two AT articles. First in 1921: The care of the countryside, which the scouting life instills, is vital to any real protection of "home and country." Already basic, it can be made spectacular. Here is something to be dramatized.'

Then in 1932:

'To learn to read first hand, on the horizon and along the stream, the big outlines of the primeval drama; to take specifically the Appalachian country as the common school and playground; . . . . this appears to be the logical second stage for the second decade of our enterprise.'

"The first job has been accomplished. The care of the Appalachian countryside has been dramatized by just such folks, Dorothy, as you. You have raised the curtain on the stage of the primeval drama itself. There, on that stage, the big show is going on, and you physically see its varied characters, bird, bug, or birch, taking their apparently aimless roles. Most of us, however, do not mentally perceive what those characters are up to, and how they are parts only of an organized, forward moving, community life.

"It remains to dramatize the drama; to bring out what the show is all about; to read between the trees and find the story of the forest. Most of us can't do it; we are illiterates when it comes to reading nature at first hand. True, we've learned our ABC's; we can tell a pine from a murmuring hemlock, and a crow from a duck; but we don't recognize their wilderness homeland as a going-concern and civilization. Our minds fail to perceive what our eyes see; we look straight at this wilderness civilization and say there ain't no such thing."

"How do we go about learning how to read nature at first hand," I asked. In answer, the Nestor handed me a reprint of his 1932 article which he calls "The Guide." "In that," said he, "I tried to state some notions on how an ignoramus like myself might teach himself to read the wilderness straight instead of printed, and to wean himself gradually from nature on a paper page to nature on the open trail. I've made some other attempts during these intervening twenty years, principally in connection with the Wilderness Society.

"Of course, there is nothing new about the outdoor study of nature; it is as old as history, and older than human history. The National Park Service is doing some fine work in this field; and I recall one or two nature walks with your PATC years ago. I hope you keep them up. They should be preceded by 'a look out the window.' Charlie Thomas gave me such a look the other evening at your headquarters, in that fine display of maps and the detailed profile of the Range. Here you combine play and school.

"Human contact with the outdoors, call it recreation or education or conservation or what you will, is, I believe, ripe for a new approach. Take your Appalachian playground from Maine to Georgia.

Here is a chance to do for wilderness history what you actually did do for wilderness geography, namely, fit the parts together in one big whole. There were separate trails north and separate trails south as well as in between; each had its separate geography; and you fitted them all together in one geography, that of the Appalachian Trail. In every section on this Trail, in every valley leading from its crest, there are hundreds of separate objects of interest to be seen or found; there are birds overhead, worms, underfoot, trees and waterfalls between; each has its separate history, its special role to play. As with the separate trails, so with these separate roles, you can fit them all together in one big history, the drama of the Appalachian Wilderness. In this way you dramatize the unseen drama.

"Now you should ask me what is the use of such an approach? My first answer would be that it would compound the fun of tramping the Trail. That alone would be sufficient answer. But I'll add a hard-boiled answer. Not until there is broader cultural interest in nature and its processes shall we stir true economic interest in the conservation of nature's resources. This is something that must be tackled from both ends. It is not enough to have skilled experts in Washington, however great their know-how. There must also be know-what on the part of the folks themselves dwelling throughout the land. All the State's budgets and all the State's men can never set up a Humpty Dumpty country again, until know-how at the top is met halfway by know-what on the ground. For economic reasons, then, as well as, cultural, we need widespread literacy in terms of the open book.

"Well, we've gone back to the beginning of the century and we'd have to go forward to its close, perhaps, before these notions, now just budding with the naturalists, might get truly sprouting. If PATC does as finely by the next quarter century as by the one just closed, we'll be well upon our way. Let me speak again my admiration for the deeds that mark your milestone, and my appreciation of your interest in the early efforts leading to them."

Happy Days for the Guidebook

April 1932

Guide to Paths in the Blue Ridge, the Club's own guidebook to the long section of the Appalachian Trail between the Susquehana River and North Carolina, was published on December 15th last. In the short interval since, the book has been so enthusiastically received that its edition of 500 is almost exhausted. Factors in this gratifying result have been the loyal support of our members, who have very generally taken advantage of the below-cost price to them to secure copies, their recommendation of the book to their outdoor-minded friends, and its widespread purchase by the public. This general sale has undoubtedly been stimulated and continued by the succession of favorable and even flattering reviews of the compact little volume which have appeared and are still appearing in influential newspapers, weeklies, outdoor magazines, and other periodicals from New England to Colorado. The Club as an organization may indeed take pride in these appraisals of our publication by strangers, not one of whom, so far as known, has uttered a single adverse criticism. *The Boston Transcript*, in the very stronghold of mountain hiking, printed a laudatory appreciation. *The New York Times,* in a Sunday edition, praised it in a special editorial, an honor not accorded one book, perhaps, in a year. American Forests, in its elaborate Bicentennial Edition for February, included a very flattering review signed by the editor. Numerous nature magazines have done likewise, and even country newspapers have joined the welcome chorus, all of which is reflected in the steady flow of orders. Needless to say, this is all very gratifying to the Guidebook Committee and the Council, who see the work and cost of the enterprise so generously rewarded in the growing prominence and prestige of our Club. Incidentally, it carries a reminder to those who think of securing a copy of the Guidebook before they are all gone, not to delay much longer in doing so.

New Guidebook Ready

January 1934

At its Annual Meeting the Club expects to have ready for distribution its second edition of *Guide to Paths in the Blue Ridge.* The first edition (1930), which won enthusiastic praise from Club members and public and received favorable reviews from more than twenty magazines and a special editorial from the *New York Times,* is long since out of print.

The present revised and enlarged edition is rendered necessary by the completion of data for the many miles of the Appalachian Trail across Maryland and in southern Virginia, relocation of the trail in the central Shenandoah National Park area, the acquisition of new Club shelters, the development of several hundred miles of important side trails, and the preparation of additional chapters of great interest. As to all this matter, the original issue is obsolete.

The new edition is one-third larger than the old, contains new and essential trail data and other matter, many more illustrations, and offers twenty-one splendid maps, including large-scale loose maps covering all trails in the entire Shenandoah National Park area. It has been two years in preparation. It is believed that no finer mountain guidebook has ever been published.

This book, of which the Club may well be proud, will be sold to members at cost, to others at $3.00 a copy. Many inquiries as to when it will be obtainable have already been received. Watch for it at the Annual Meeting.

1932 Annual Meeeting

April 1932
Anonymous

The Annual Meeting of the Club was held in the auditorium of the Wilson Teachers College on the evening of January 14. The rap of President Avery's gavel brought the meeting to order and the reports of the various officers and committees were heard.

After the completion of the business program Mr. Horace Albright, Director of the National Park Service, spoke briefly.

Dr. Roy Lyman Sexton exhibited a reel of pictures showing the beauties of Isle Royale, our proposed National Park.

Mr. Philip Martindale, Chief Ranger in Yellowstone Park, one of the most colorful members of the ranger staff of our great national park, told some interesting incidents which he had experienced and showed a reel of pictures.

Dr. H. S. Hedges, of Charlottesville, in charge of the Appalachian Trail from Swift Run Gap to the southern terminus of the Virginia section, was present bringing greeting from the southern group.

The reports of officers and committees were as follows:

Report of the President
Myron H Avery

The purpose of this, my Fourth Annual Report to the Potomac Appalachian Trail Club, is to comment upon the Club activities of the past year and to note the tendencies of these activities, both actual and contemplated. We are endeavoring to build here, not a temporary organization of three, four, or five years, but to lay the foundations for a permanent organization, which, with the establishment of the Shenandoah National Park, will represent for the Central Appalachians what that Appalachian Mountain Club does for New England. That our activities for the past year should contribute to permanence is, therefore, a source of much satisfaction.

The Guidebook

Our primary contribution, not only to our membership but also to all persons interested in the outdoors, is our *Guide to the Paths in the Blue Ridge,* All of you know of this work, and the book requires no comment. I would say, however, that its appearance has been well publicized, and the book has been and will be extensively reviewed. As an organization production, all Club members will take pride in this publication. The Guidebook Editor has developed what no other similar book has evolved; that is, a concise, uniform, guidebook phraseology.

The Trail

The second permanent development is in our Trail. Most gratifying has been the marked increase in interest and activity in trail construction and maintenance as such. Last year was discouragingly lean. There is a spirit of rivalry among the various Trail Overseers. The responsible attitude of each overseer toward his section of the Trail is very gratifying to the Supervisor who has, in fact, under his jurisdiction a far-flung stretch extending 260 miles from the Susquehanna River to Rockfish Gap. The Club is primarily a trail-cutting organization, and the response to the first work trip scheduled in Maryland, when 58 people marked and opened 10 miles of

Maryland Work Trip, 1932

trail of "boulevard proportions," shows that the Club membership as a whole is interested in the trail-construction phase and not in mere hiking.

The Bulletin

Our third line of progress has been in the marked improvement in the *Club Bulletin*, for which we hold the Bulletin Editor solely responsible. The Bulletin is now established as a printed quarterly, and with the increase in activity and knowledge of the regions through which our Trail passes, we can expect continued expansion in this direction.

Shelters

A year ago, we announced the Club's intention of maintaining the Sexton Shelter fully equipped with cooking utensils, bedding, and other necessary apparatus. Our plan has been realized with the exception of what seems an unnecessary deficiency of bedding. Both the Sexton and Meadow Spring shelters have been used extensively and have been a source of very real pleasure to Club members. As soon as the Club's financial condition permits, two additional bunks should be provided for the Sexton Shelter. It is interesting to note that the receipts from outsiders who have used the shelter, without any inconvenience to Club members, have equaled the cost of maintaining and adding to the equipment of the Sexton Shelter. The presence of these two structures has only served to emphasize to the Club the necessity for additional shelters, particularly in the region between Thornton and Chester Gaps. We have necessarily been forced to postpone any actual construction until we could determine the burden on the Club's finances which the issuing of the Guidebook would involve. This is now behind us, and we are in a position to proceed promptly with the plans developed by the Shelters Committee for two or three new structures of the closed cabin or open shelter type. The next year should see our present shelter system increased to at least five.

Equipment Bulletin

In addition to developing among the Club membership a familiarity with the Blue Ridge region, it has been a part of our program to make available to Club members information as to useful items of hiking and camping equipment. For this purpose, the Club has issued two editions of a printed bulletin listing a wide variety of hiking and camping equipment and giving precise information for articles required for trips in the Blue Ridge region, but avoiding any discussion as to relative merits of the various items, which is much a matter of personal preference.

Club Trips

A year ago, we commenced an experiment in the conduct of our Club trips. The average attendance on the monthly trips, which in some instances has run as high as 70, made it impossible to continue the monthly trips by private cars. It was also impossible to schedule such trips as the Appalachian Trail Hike Series. The burden of arranging private-car trips for parties of this size is obviously too much to ask of the hike leaders. So the bus trip has become a fixed part of our program. The cost, of course, somewhat exceeds that of trips made by private cars, but the attendance on the bus trips and the expressions of satisfaction show that the system has met with general approval in the Club. The advantages are obvious and, for most members, outweigh the increased cost. The Excursions Committee, under the direction of its energetic chairman, Walter R. Jex, has endeavored in these trips to provide for the participation of as many Club members as possible and to provide for as much variety as an average of ten trips a year affords. The system of long and short hikes on the same trip is a satisfactory instance of this planning.

The Summer Camps

The attendance at the Club's Smoky Mountain Camp shows that the membership wishes an opportunity to visit outstanding scenic regions at low cost. Such trips would otherwise be impossible except to a very limited few. In the future such camps will be scheduled during the regular vacation season. The 1932 Camp in the White Mountains in August will afford an opportunity to become familiar with the best developed outdoor recreational region in the East. All our active trail workers should become familiar with the Appalachian Mountain Club hut and trail system.

Participation in Club Activities

In building for permanence, the policy of the Council has been to spread participation in Club activities as far as possible, with the particular thought of familiarizing interested workers with the Club's program, so that they may assume its responsibilities and its offices. The nature of the Club organization requires that its business be conducted largely by the Council, but the committee chairmen have been requested to attend many Council meetings, and in this way quite an extensive group participate in the Club's management. I have commented before upon this policy. You will have noticed each year the addition of new officers and committees with very definite work and responsibilities. A particular example is the pending development of an Excursions Committee of 10 or 12 members, with the purpose of developing trained and responsible leaders for Club trips.

Maps

My last report noted a deficiency along the line of maps. This deficiency was happily remedied in time to provide the Skyland insert map in the Guidebook, and our troubles in this connection are at an end.

Cooperation with Other Groups

With some pride, we feel that this Club has had much to do with the development, within the past year and a half, of the very active organization to the south of us, so that there is no break in the Trail.

We hope to be able to develop similar groups in Maryland and southern Pennsylvania. Individuals of the Club, cooperating with Forester Bradley of Mont Alto, and Assistant Forester Norris of Michaux Forest, marked the trail in southern Pennsylvania. We have responsibility for this section. The Supervisor would like to allocate the South Mountain section to responsible overseers.

Present Objects

Our present objects, therefore, seem to be the completion of the remaining 25 miles of the 40-mile Trail across Maryland, which promises to be a reality this summer; the location of two or three additional shelters; continued work in gathering Guidebook data for side trails and newly opened regions; and increased efforts to develop scientific and historic data for the region which is our playground. Articles in the Guidebook reflect activity in this direction, and we hope to greatly increase it.

Stenographic Help Needed

We have one very particular need. The typing of Guidebook data and other Club material involves much stenographic labor. Three Club members, Misses Pomeroy, Kempt, and Krause, have of late borne the burden of this work. We are sure that there are others who would gladly help, and we ask that they indicate their willingness to Miss Fulkerson.

Shenandoah National Park History

Corbin Hollow School, 1932

Skyland Before 1900

by Jean Stephenson
July 1935

Skyland is a comparatively recent but very appropriate name for the central point of one of the most interesting sections of the northern Virginia Blue Ridge, that between Thornton Gap and Fishers Gap. Here, for the first time south of Vermont, the eastern mountain ridge reaches an elevation of 1,000 feet, with sheer cliffs facing the Great Valley to the west.

It is not surprising that the Indians thought these peaks, so often veiled in mist, were the abiding place of the Great Spirit.

It was only a little over two hundred years ago that the white man first attempted to occupy these hills. Since that time their history has been an interesting one. The history of this region is an epitome of the history of the nation. Frenzied land speculation, settlement, emigration, land litigation, mining ventures, isolation, indiscriminate destruction of game and national resources all played a part. The people still remaining live as their forefathers lived, using the quaint speech of over a century ago. Their ancestors, descended from the best blood of the British Isles, settled in this mountain land then abounding in game, fruit and nut trees, and magnificent timber. Cut off from communication by lack of roads, generation after generation has seen the game disappear, the fruit trees die, the timber cut off and the lands exploited by outsiders, after which the fertile soil washed away; yet the people cling to their lands, even though it is now taken over by the Park Authorities. Soon they will have to go. But if they can be located in not too unfamiliar surroundings and can overcome their nostalgia for their mountain tops and adjust themselves to new conditions, sufficient food may make the next generation of this group a decided asset to the State.

As early as 1712, Larkin Chew and Augustine Smith, leading planters of Essex and King and Queen Counties, secured from the Governor of Virginia large grants of land stretching up into the mountains. Gradually it was sold. Between 1724 and 1726 many Germans from

Governor Spotswood's German Colony settled at the mouth of White Oak Run (now called "canyon"), then known as Island Run from the island at its mouth. Their descendants are still in the community.

About 1730, James Barbour purchased from the heirs of Smith much of the mountain land, and himself secured patents for additional land in the vicinity. It was divided into small tracts of 50, 100, and 150 acres, and disposed of to many from the Tidewater sections of Virginia and to a few recent arrivals of French and German extraction. At that time the mountain land was quite desirable, but within a generation it was found that tracts so small could not support large families. So many moved away to North and South Carolina and Georgia, from whence in another generation they went on to Kentucky, Tennessee, and the west. In some cases other, took their places; in some, the land relapsed to the wilderness.

In 1796, James Barbour had a survey made of the lands he still owned or that had reverted to him from below the Conway River to Thornton Gap and from half way across the Hazel plateau to west of the crest line of the Ridge. This is known as "The Big Survey." Soon after another real estate boom resulted in another influx of settlers.

Meanwhile Lord Fairfax had made grants south from his Gooney Run Manor to below Swift Run Gap, which of course included the same territory as that covered by the Chew-Smith-Barbour grants. Patents covering the Fairfax grants changed hands many times, and even after the settlement of the Northern Neck boundary dispute, the holders claimed land south of the Rappahannock. The controversies between these rival claimants, purchasers at tax sales, and the actual occupants consumed the time of the courts for many years between 1820 and 1855. Hardly had these been settled when the Civil War and reconstruction period with its aftermath of tax sales caused new confusion. As a result of all this, the "mountain people" came to view with suspicion all "furriners," and the attempts to enforce laws providing for heavy taxation of whiskey, the only real industry in the mountains, only intensified this feeling.

One of the reasons for the interest of nonresidents of the State in these lands was due to the widely established belief that valuable ores were to be found. The Indians secured copper for their axes and ornaments from Stony Man; and during colonial days many attempts at mining were made. From 1850 to 1860, large sums were expended on prospecting, and many companies organized for this purpose. One deed shows the consideration for the sale of 63 acres to be one million dollars, but it appears only $8,000 was actually paid. Furnace Spring, near Skyland. provided the water used for mining operations on Stony Man. Traces can still be seen of the copper refuse and of the charcoal pits used in making charcoal for smelting the ore. The old shaft, 60 feet deep, filled up with water long ago. In Dark Hollow, below Fishers Gap, were the most extensive workings. Ore from this mine was taken over the mountain at Fishers Gap and down the switchback road to Stanley.

One of the owners of the Stony Man Mining Company was Mr. George H. Pollock. In 1887 his son, Mr. G. Freeman Pollock, visited the region, then almost inaccessible, as there was no road on Stony Man, only a trail. He realized that it would be a wonderful recreation place and soon thereafter the Blue Ridge Stony Man Park came into being. Later Mr. Pollock founded here the mountain resort, Skyland, and did much to interest people in the natural beauties of this area. Skyland will in the future be the center of the Shenandoah Park activities.

The name given one of the most noted trails in the vicinity, the Passamaquoddy, is a play on Mr. Pollock's name. It is a Maine Indian word meaning "abounding in pollock." Thornton Gap preserves the name of Francis Thornton, who as early as 1733 built a home in F. T. Valley (so called from his initials), and whose land ran far up the hollow. The story goes that he brought his bride, the beautiful Mary Savage, from Westmoreland County, and one day they rode to the top of the Great Pass Mountain, then climbed the rocks on the summit, from which be pointed out his land and presented it to her. In commemoration of this, and because she was the first white woman to climb the mountain, the "rock pile" on top was called after her, "Mary's Rock." After her husband's death, the land on this mountain and in this gap was given her as dower and long known as "Madam Thornton's Quarter." As early as 1763, a road was cut from here through "the Hazel Wilderness," and it is still used, and known as

"Hazel Road." One of the Trail Club's shelters is located at the place described in deeds of a century and a quarter ago as "the meadow spring, near Marys Rock on the Great Pass Mountain." The name "Great Pass Mountain" has faded from the maps, but "Marys Rock" is widely known and the shelter is "Meadow Spring Shelter."

Why Skyland?

by G. Freeman Pollock

The question "Why Skyland?" will undoubtedly be of great interest to the public, because if there had been no Skyland, then there would be no Shenandoah National Park.

Along about 1845-50 there was a copper boom in the area now selected for the park. Quite a number of companies were organized to investigate and explore the region for copper indications. The few copper companies which had been created before that time had made little progress. In 1850 the Miners' Lode Copper Company, Inc., with stockholders mostly from New York and vicinity, began operation on the so-called Stony Man Mountain properties, consisting of 5,371 acres.

Among the stockholders were Stephen M. Allen, of Boston, President of the Massachusetts Historical Society, whose son, Horace G. Allen, was Speaker of the House of Delegates at Boston at one time; and my father, George H. Pollock, an importer, of Salem, Massachusetts.

Of the various operations conducted at different points, the principal one was mining on a small scale just a few hundred yards northeast of Stony Man Peak. The ore was shot through the native copper, making it very hard to work.

The present site of Skyland was the point selected for the smelting of the ore. The name Furnace Spring was given to the spring where the smelting plant was located. To this day, considerable slag and other materials can be found there. The open field was at that time heavily timbered, and charcoal was made at Furnace Field, where the tennis courts are now. The ore was carried on muleback from the mine around back of the Peak to the furnaces. The machinery, which was evidently very simple, was brought from the foot of the mountain over a single horseback trail, constructed by the miners, which was then called the Jones's Slide Road, so named because of a very steep place near the summit where the mules had to come over solid rock in a sort of gutter.

This copper mine proved to be worthless, like most of the others in this area, and the pocket of ore on Stony Man Peak had been worked out even before the Civil War put an end to all operations in the Blue Ridge for that generation. The company also owned the so-called Dark Hollow Copper Mine in Madison County at Haywood Mountain. This tract of land contained some 5,000 acres. Thus, about 1850, Pollock and Allen, through their holdings in the Miners' Lode Copper Company, were actual owners of some 10,000 acres of land, or one-sixteenth of the entire area of the Shenandoah National Park.

When I was four years old, my family moved to Washington, D.C. Because the climate did not agree with me, I was sent at the age of ten to a farm at Weston, Massachusetts, where the Pollock family had formerly lived. I worked on the farm and was educated there until I was strong and healthy enough to return to Washington to attend the public schools. It was the intention of the family to educate me as all the others had been educated, to enter the teaching profession, but I had no liking for that and resisted, and, I am afraid, became a rather bad boy, stealing off to go hunting, fishing, camping or just to get out into the woods, frequently with only Dicky Daddles, the dog, for company. Efforts to interest me in business failed, for I decided that I wanted to become a naturalist in order to get out into the open and succeeded in interesting William T. Hornaday, then Chief Taxidermist of the National Museum, who gave me work under William Palmer and his father, two of the best taxidermists in the country. After I had been some two years with Dr. Hornaday, my father told me, in a serious talk, of his stock holdings in Virginia properties which he had never seen but which he thought would be excellent country for hunting. This sounded like an adventure of discovery. After receiving permission from Dr. Hornaday and obtaining what little information Mr. Allen had secured for me in Boston giving the location of the properties, I started out in October, 1886 at the age of sixteen, with my collecting outfit, shotgun, and dog for Page County, Virginia, with no further information than that this property was located on a mountain called Stony Man Mountain. On my arrival at Luray, a search was made among numerous families by the name of Prince for one which had boarded some miners thirty-five years before. It was learned at the home of John Dave Prince, near the foot of Stony Man Mountain, that his father had boarded the miners for several seasons. Mr. Prince knew of the location of what was called the Stony Man Mountain Big Survey, but beyond that nothing was known about ownership. The entire property had been used and despoiled by practically everybody living in the vicinity. The mountaineers had squatted on the land and were "wild and woolly" back in the hollows, particularly in what was known as Free State Hollow. It was said that it was called "Free State" because, for excellent reasons, sheriffs and deputy sheriffs stayed out and the people practically ruled themselves. Everybody in that section near the foot of the mountains on the western slope of the ridge, Sam Sours, Peter Sours, the Somerses, Princes, Burrackers, Woodwards, Prices, was getting bark, wood, poles, lumber, anything off the land, and had been for many years. On the eastern slopes and in the hollows, the mountain people lived off the Pollock lands, and, with the exception of one or two, did not even claim to have title.

Many stories were told me of rattlesnakes and "hoop snakes," a deadly species which was supposed to roll down the hill directly toward you (after putting its tail into its mouth and making its body rigid to form a wheel), then at the proper distance to strike you with his tail, which meant death in agony. In fact, dignified old men told me solemnly that even large oak trees, when struck by accident by these "hoop snakes," withered and died before night.

I looked forward to all sorts of adventure on my first expedition to Stony Man Peak, with only John D. Price and Dicky Daddles, the dog, for company. On the way we met several wild-looking mountain men, first Merrity Dodson, very thin and pale, with deep-set sunken blue eyes, light hair, bare feet (even though it was October), who showed every appearance of poverty. He was dragging down the mountain two chestnut ties. This was my first sight of a mountain man.

Mr. Prince cleared his throat with much solemnity and said, "Merrity, I want you to meet Mr. Pollock, owner of the Big Survey on which you all live. Mr. Pollock's father has owned this land way back before your mountain days, and his son has come to look it over to see what can be done about selling the land or getting something out of it in some way. He is friendly to you all and wants to meet you all." Merrity Dodson did not answer. However, as he stood there above us, his blue eyes carefully scrutinized me from head to foot. Without saying "How do you do," or "Goodbye," or "God bless you," he started down the hill, dragging the ties after him, and disappeared.

Only the year before, Merrity Dodson had been one of a group of mountain men and women who had gathered together as a means of protection in the so-called Parks Cabin, which was located about a mile from Skyland. There is a most interesting story connected with this event, which resulted in the murder of an officer on the evening in question at the Parks Cabin. Merrity Dodson, I believe, was at the time of our meeting the only one of the five men in the group not in the penitentiary for this murder.

As we continued our trip up the mountain, Mr. Prince told me this story, further impressing upon me the uncivilized nature of the section. However, the rattlesnakes were not as plentiful as pictured, for we encountered only one, and its unexciting death at the hands of Mr. Prince was not disappointing.

The wind blew hard and the air was cold, but we soon reached the peak. To say that I was carried away with the magnificent view, the first extensive one I had ever seen except from hilltops at Harpers Ferry, is putting it mildly. I raved and shouted and probably would have yodeled, if I had known at that time how to yodel. Truly it seemed like a fairy story. John Dave Prince smiled benevolently and agreed that it was a grand sight. It was evident that, except for a few of the farmers near the foot of the mountain, no travelers had ever visited this section. After reveling in the marvelous panorama for some ten or fifteen minutes, we decided that as we were very hungry, we would eat the bread and butter and jelly which we had brought for lunch; but woe unto us! The dog had got ahead of us and was just smacking his lips over the last few morsels. So, we had no lunch.

There you have the story of the real discovery of this marvelous area by one who, from that moment henceforth, made it his business to "tell the world," and I certainly did. Returning to Washington without doing any collecting, that was too trivial, I described the wonders I had seen and the possibilities which would result from bringing this area to the attention of the world. My father and three or four of his friends, though incredulous, had enough curiosity to make the trip to see what it was all about. They were all as thrilled as I had been. They realized that great possibilities were there even though they had seen nothing but the peak itself, and returned to Washington to spread the news of this discovery. My father immediately communicated with Stephen M. Allen in Boston, and together they spent the winter in perfecting their title to the 5,371-acre tract, which included Stony Man Mountain, a portion of Thoroughfare Mountain, Hot Mountain, also some of Hazel Mountain, a goodly portion of Hawksbill and all of Millers Head and Bushy Top, all of Dry Run Canyon, a portion of the headwaters of White Oak Canyon, and more.

Mr. Allen and my father decided to develop this property as a resort, and the following summer, while they worked out their plans, a friend of mine, William Wallace Deane of Washington, and I arranged to spend the season alone camping on the little plateau formerly described as Furnace Field. Once a week Herbert Prince, the son of John D. Prince, came up with a basket of food, fresh country bread baked in the old brick oven, eggs, bacon, tomatoes, apples, potatoes, butter, and some good country-cured ham. This was our diet for the summer, and I was the cook because I liked the job. William Wallace Deane is a well-known patent attorney in Washington today.

During the next winter, arrangements were made to survey a town site on the site of Furnace Field and to sell lots, the receipts from which were to be used to develop the property, build a road, and pay off a mortgage on the property. A few lots were sold, and Smith Sherman, Chief Engineer of the Luray Tanneries and a professional mountain road builder, was employed to survey and lay off the road. Then John Dave Prince was hired as construction foreman. However, because the road as planned was estimated to cost more money than would become available immediately, the survey was not strictly adhered to, which accounts for the very steep and sheer winds in the road.

As soon as the roadwork was begun, I became more ambitious, and succeeded in interesting my friend Harry English, Professor of

Mathematics in the Washington High School, and Fletcher Kearney, a Virginian, in the formation of a company that would get stumpage from my father and Mr. Allen in order to go into the mill business on the top of Stony Man Mountain and begin building. There was a boom going on at this time in all the towns in the valleys of Virginia, and lots in small places like Luray were being sold to northern people at fabulous prices. To this day in Luray some of the better parts of the town are still referred to as "Boomfield." Our prospects looked bright, and we founded the business firm of Kearney, English, and Pollock, Mill Owners, Builders, and Contractors, and owners of the Blue Ridge Park Livery Stables.

We had no trouble in buying all the machinery we needed, but the difficulty came in transporting the machinery to the top of the mountain, as at this time the road was only about one-fourth completed. Consequently, the huge engine actually had to be hauled the entire distance from the foot of the mountain to Stony Man Peak by using ten to twelve horses pulling downhill, with pulleys arranged to carry the machinery up the hill! At last this feat was accomplished and a well-equipped mill was built about 300 yards below Furnace Spring at the point where the present bridge crosses Dry Run to the entrance to Passamaquoddy Trail.

During the summer and part of the winter, work was carried on. English could not participate actively in the management of the company because of his teaching position in Washington. Kearney and I spent the winter in a shanty located directly on the cliff near the present tennis courts. As a protection against depredations by the mountaineers at night, I obtained a number of very valuable large dogs, two marvelous greyhounds, King Richard and Lady Vivian, prize winners imported from England, and four English mastiffs, including Old Dutch, who at one time was first-prize winner at Crystal Palace Dog Show in London. One of the mastiffs was known as the worst dog in all Washington. Because of the very cold weather, kennels were built by digging pits in the ground four feet deep and then erecting a small log-cabin type of structure from the bottom of the pit to a point about three feet above ground. After roofing this little building, the whole thing was covered with a couple of feet of earth, so that in the snow these dog kennels looked like Eskimo huts. The dogs entered the kennels by openings under the ground. They were kept in during the day, but at night were turned loose and gave excellent protection. We fed them extremely well and trained them not to eat food offered by others, with the result that they were not poisoned. Occasionally when the man in charge of the dogs overlooked putting them in the kennels for the day, mountaineers had to take to the trees for safety.

Our firm expected to make money by the manufacture of necessary building material and the erection of buildings for the development of the properties by a stock company called the Blue Ridge Park Association, organized by my father, Mr. Allen, and a John Bowles, Washington real estate man. About the time we got started, however, my father and Mr. Allen became convinced that the Blue Ridge Park Association would result more in a moneymaking scheme for the directors than in providing funds for development, and they refused to continue with the company. The following winter, after we had proceeded to mill a good supply of material, the Association sued Pollock and Allen for fulfillment of contract and obtained injunctions preventing them from selling stumpage to us until the suit was settled. This stopped all millwork, and our little firm was left high and dry with indebtedness staring us in the face, a distracting situation. The legal battle was fought in the Page County courts at Luray, with the result that Pollock and Allen won the suit.

Beginnings of Shenandoah National Park

by G. Freeman Pollock
April 1937

So many fragmentary, garbled, and even wholly erroneous accounts of the genesis of the now famous Shenandoah National Park have appeared from various sources in recent years that the true narrative of all events which resulted in it, with sufficient of their background to make the picture complete, appears to be timely.

The Potomac Appalachian Trail Club, so intimately interested in the Park area, has asked me for the whole story. This, in all its details, could not be told in many issues of the Club *Bulletin.* The most important facts, many of which seemed to us dramatic as they occurred, can be more briefly set forth, however, and I consider it a duty, and will make it my pleasure, to do this. They were all well known to many people at the time, of course, but probably are still remembered in their entirety by few, and it may be well to state them in that way here once for all.

In 1920, my wife, Mrs. George Freeman Pollock, financed the purchase for $1,000 from a man named Grim in Stanley, Va., of the choicest of the still standing hemlock trees at the so-called Limberlost Swamp, near Skyland but not located on my land, to keep them from being destroyed. The idea in our minds at that time was that some day, sooner or later, this area would be used for public recreation purposes. We had no idea, however, of a federal park or even of a state park, in saving these trees. On the other hand, I had for some time been considering getting some Congressmen interested in the locality; it was with this general idea in mind that I spent so much time and effort in trying to preserve it from fire. For years previously I had consulted with friends and owners of adjoining tracts, trying to obtain cooperation in preserving the district from fire and the ax.

In the thirty-five years I had lived at Skyland, time and again I had fought fires at my own expense, hoping that eventually some arrangement could be made to preserve White Oak Canyon in particular. I am happy to say that it was saved from fire many times by my own personal efforts; I suppose that I must have expended something like $3,500 in fighting forest fires throughout a period of over thirty years. No assistance was forthcoming on these occasions; on the contrary, not only the mountain people, but sometimes the valley farmers as well would, instead of helping put out the fires, go to their fences and set new fires to prevent their own fences from being burned down, thus spreading the fire in all directions.

On one occasion, my fire watchman, whom I had on the lookout especially during the spring and fall of every year, wired me at Roanoke, where I had just arrived with two friends on a walking trip on which we had walked the entire distance from Skyland to Roanoke. Footsore and weary from this long walk, I had not been in the hotel four hours until his message came that forest fires threatened Skyland in all directions. I hurried back. This, I believe, was the first fire I ever fought. It lasted several days, and although we controlled it more or less and steered it around in various directions, saving Kettle Canyon by a miracle and White Oak Canyon as well on that occasion, there is no telling what damage would finally have been done but for a providential rain. I had gangs from the nearby towns and from the valley and the foot of the mountain, but very little help of any kind from the mountaineers. Mine was all paid help except a gang that came up from the livery stable in Luray and about ten farmer friends who helped for a day in the Skyland Road group. It was necessary to keep racing on horseback from one danger point to another, directing and encouraging the separated groups of fire fighters, with practically no rest or sleep in the meantime. When the fire was extinguished after the third or fourth day, there were about three hundred men in my employ. One gang of some fifty men were kept along the old Skyland Road, which saved Kettle Canyon. The story of this fire and how it was fought is indeed thrilling. Because of the high wind and a dry season, the terrifying flames, although we fought them valiantly, very nearly destroyed Skyland. We saved hundreds of young fir balsam trees in the Hawksbill area. The Limberlost Swamp was also saved from being burned. It was years after this spectacular fire before our county had a force of firefighting men; but even after the fire protection system was inaugurated, fire wardens would call on Skyland for assistance, and I would send as many men as I could get and would pay them myself, since there were no funds to pay them otherwise.

An important part in preventing this part of the Blue Ridge from being exploited by lumber companies was also played at Skyland. Every few years some new company would come along that was willing to go into the lumber business provided they could get from 15,000 to 20,000 acres. They wanted principally to get hold of the Cedar Run Tract, the Christadora Tract and Number Three Tract of the Big Survey which belonged to me; but always they declared that unless they could get the entire area, it would not pay to build roads and put in other facilities necessary to get the lumber out. The moment I heard that such a deal was on foot I would immediately arrange to throw a monkeywrench into the machinery and break up the proceeding; I was successful in doing this over and over again, and made quite a few enemies in the process. Numerous times, timber cruisers went over the property and came back with various proposals to me, but for commercial timber exploitation there was simply nothing doing. It was true that I had to cut enough timber to provide firewood for Skyland, and that in the very beginning of my life in the mountains I had to assist myself by selling some chestnut bark. The felling for my personal needs, however, was trifling, and the sale of chestnut bark was necessary only to get started and was resorted to with great regret in the realization that, surrounded with thieves as I was, if I did not get this bark myself it would be taken out anyway; these bark stealers continued to steal bark for fifteen years after I arrived on the Ridge. Of course, I also knew that the white oak used in the mountaineers' basket industry was practically all taken from the so-called Big Survey; this I could not object to because this was practically the only legitimate industry of the mountaineers, and was very minor in its effect. Nevertheless, it destroyed much excellent white oak timber.

A short story serves here to show the little respect people had for property rights in the Blue Ridge. For years after we built the Stony Man Road from the foot of the mountain to Skyland, visiting farmers and residents of Luray would bring parties up the mountain on picnics, and unless you stood on that road in person and were willing to stand your ground and maintain your rights, such people would invariably cut beautiful young pine trees and tie them to the backs of the buggies to use as brakes. Not only would this destroy lovely trees growing practically in your front yard, but the branches would rake the sides of the road and drag down boulders and stones into it, making it necessary, after each picnic party, for me to send my men down over the road to throw these obstructions out. Always at the foot of the mountain there would be fine young trees lying bedraggled and dead.

The mountain people, and oftentimes valley people as well, would go through the mountains in droves, and do you think they would climb a tree to shake down chestnuts? Not at all! They were out with axes and left a path of destruction behind them, cutting down tall trees to get the chestnuts from the tops. I used to ride around when I heard this chopping and put a stop to it. Just as soon as I went back I would hear it again. Only the chestnut blight put a final and tragic end to that. To one who loved the forests and who hoped to preserve them in some way it had been an arduous and unending task to protect them to any substantial degree. At last, thank God, Stephen T. Mather and Secretary of the Interior Hubert Work came into the picture in a big way, with the untold benefits that have followed their vision. But I am getting a little ahead of my story.

Part II

The Blue Ridge land I acquired through my father had appealed to him from the standpoint of its natural resources; but instead of profiting from these, I preferred to enjoy the natural attractions of the place, which I was in love with from the beginning. This is probably the only kind of exploitation that preserves and protects instead of marring and destroying natural beauty, and since the first suggestion of a national park in the Blue Ridge was inspired by the state of nature at Skyland, and the suggestion was first "sold" to the site selection commission there, I think it can truthfully be said that the existence of Shenandoah National Park and the Skyline Drive today is due to my adherence to the fortunate decision I made thirty-five years ago.

Our good friends Mr. and Mrs. Harold Allen of Washington, D.C., had visited Skyland several times and were so enthusiastic over its scenery that they only regretted it was not more widely known and enjoyed. In February 1924 came a small *Washington Star* clipping by mail from Mr. Allen, with "Why not Skyland?" on a slip of paper attached. The clipping told of the appointment by Secretary of the Interior Work of a special commission to recommend the site for a national park in the Southern Appalachians. I was very busy, and nothing came of the matter until early in the summer when the Allens came to Skyland, but Harold Allen had kept it in mind, and before he left Washington, interviewed Colonel Glenn H. Smith, Secretary of the Commission, learned the status of the undertaking, and obtained a copy of the Government's printed questionnaire, which he brought with him to Skyland. The commission had been approached by a number of individuals and groups suggesting various sites, all unsuitable for park purposes for one reason or another. The time for their report was nearly up, and the commission was pretty well satisfied that no acceptable site was available north of the Great Smoky Mountains.

It appeared that the Massanutten Mountain area had been suggested to the Commission but was not believed to be up to National Park standard. The questionnaire, which Harold Allen urged be filled in at once, was a challenge which he pointed out the Skyland region could meet. With the benefit of his information received from Colonel Smith, he and I went into confab next morning with Mr. George H. Judd in that famous session in the Judd in "Tryst of the Winds," and dictated to my stenographer a rough draft of the information pertaining to the Skyland region which the Government wanted about proposed sites. I personally answered most of the questions as I was the only one sufficiently familiar with the area to do so. I said frankly that I was familiar with about 50,000 acres surrounding Skyland and felt sure that territory both north and south of this area could be quickly explored and undoubtedly would be found to be of the same caliber. I proposed to explore those areas at my own expense and make a further report. The answers sounded good. They actually were. We all got excited with the task as it progressed. And no wonder! Just to recount the natural features of the region convinced us that we had a real national park site to present, and were perhaps making history that very moment in doing so.

The time limit was so nearly up that Harold Allen left with the precious papers forthwith for Washington, where he condensed the rough draft, had the questionnaire typed up and, not trusting the United States mail, handed it himself to Colonel Smith with an earnest statement to the effect that, "This has been prepared by responsible people who know the facts they present. *It is all true.* When you have read it you will see that it will be impossible for the commission not to come and inspect the Skyland region." This last statement also turned out to be true, but not without some further oral persuasion.

A few days later I read in a Winchester paper an article by the Honorable Thomas W. Harrison of Front Royal, Va., Member of Congress, describing the Massanutten area and stating that an organization known as Shenandoah Valley, Inc., was promoting that site and seeking to have the commission recommend it as suitable for a national park. I got in touch with Harold Allen, and we studied this article and agreed that these people were working on the wrong track and that Virginia should get behind something much finer than the Massanutten project. We made an appointment with Mr. Hugh Naylor of Front Royal, who was at the head of Shenandoah Valley, Inc., promoters of the Massanutten site, to show us the points of interest in it. A few days later, Mr. and Mrs. Allen, Mr. and Mrs. Ferdinand Zerkel of Luray, Mrs. Pollock and I met Mr. Naylor and were taken to see what this area offered. We drove into the Fort Valley from Front Royal and came out at Strasburg. Even in this brief excursion it was obvious that comparison with the Blue Ridge was absurd, and we also quickly saw that there was no chance for this area being considered seriously by the commission.

Knowing that Ferdinand Zerkel was an important member of Shenandoah Valley, Inc., I made an appointment with him to meet me at the Page Valley National Bank in Luray on a matter of great importance. He met me, and in the presence of Mr. Emmit Berry, cashier of the bank, I talked for an hour like a wild man. The point was that with their organization already set up, this was a fine opportunity for them to take up the Blue Ridge proposition and drop the Massanutten at once. I explained that the park finding commission could see without walking out of Colonel Glenn Smith's office, by examining topographic maps, that the Massanutten area offered no attractions for a national park. Mr. Berry and Mr. Zerkel could not help being impressed with my argument, but the organization was already definitely committed to the Massanutten area. Action had to be quick as the commission had just about finished its visits and nothing acceptable north of the Great Smokies had been seen. I clinched my argument with, "Why continue, only because you are committed to it, advocating something which you know to be a foredoomed failure? Why not get on the band wagon with a movement that promises to be a success?" This seemed to strike the nail on the head, and when I asked Mr. Zerkel where I could get in touch with Shenandoah Valley, Inc., and he replied, "At Harrisonburg." I shouted, "Let's call them up. Let me talk to them." Mr. Dan Wine, Secretary of Shenandoah Valley, Inc., was quickly reached and I told him that I had some information relative to the National Park situation of such immediate importance that I would like to have him call a meeting of as many of the members of his organization as could be gathered.

The Shenandoah Scenery

From *American Civic Annual,* 1930
by Harold Allen

Editor's Note: The Southern Appalachian National Park Commission recommended a National Park in the Blue Ridge Mountains, named for the famous Shenandoah Valley below. Congress has authorized the Secretary of the Interior to accept the Park as soon as sufficient area is acquired. Harold Allen was the first to propose a National Park in the Shenandoah. As Councilor of the Potomac Appalachian Trail Club, he has explored the remote valleys and the high peaks of the region. The Club (a constituent of the Appalachian Trail Conference described last year by Judge Perkins) has already cut more than 100 miles of skyline trail to give access to the Park. The charming account which Mr. Allen has sent us is like a mellow water-color which has caught the evanescent beauty of sky and stream and mount and vale. As a companion piece we present Dr. Sexton's account of the forgotten people of the region remote from all evidences of civilization though so near the Nation's capital. There is a frontier in the Blue Ridge Mountains which has its roots in the dim past, far back of the cowboy period of the western plains.

———————

SCENERY, so often described in easy terms of comparison, can often better be represented in terms of contrast. "The Switzerland of America," "Niagara of the West," and similar phrases bring indulgent smiles, from the knowledge that the originals could probably be more accurately distinguished from their supposed counterparts than likened to them. For the face of nature, presents an infinite variety of types between coast and prairie, crag and forest, that makes landscapes individual and supplies a grateful diversity to man's outlook on his physical world. No two sections really look very much alike. Topography, geology, climate, water or its absence, and vegetation all combine to paint the special picture. Even the dwellers in it play their part, for to the observing eye are they not the foreground, so to speak, of every characteristic scene?

So, in gazing down the mountain range or into the lovely valleys of the Shenandoah National Park, we shall not see the Adirondacks of the South, because in spite of other similarities, the familiar lakes are missing, but the quite distinctive and altogether entrancing Blue Ridge Mountains of Virginia.

A wild and unknown country to the bold adventurers whom Governor Spotswood led across it in 1716, they remain strangely unfamiliar to the generation of today. The Shenandoah National Park, so certain of realization that it can be referred to as a present fact, will make the beauties of this region familiar to millions of eastern city dwellers and preserve the enjoyment of them to posterity. A mere intimation of its attractions can be set forth here.

Although the Blue Ridge averages fully as high above its surrounding country as the Rockies, the outlook of 60 miles down its spurred and buttressed chain from the summit of Mary's Rock, highest peak at the Park's northern end, is nearly all a view of sweeping lines and molded contours. It is as though these mountains, vastly older geologically than their western brothers, had time to mellow and soften through eons of prehistory into a gracious beauty planned by Nature to appeal to man. Their slopes and summits are clothed with a prodigal range of vegetation, including more than fifty varieties of trees. From the first breath of spring until the chilling winds of winter, they are garlanded with blooming shrubs and flowers.

The South Shenandoah Valley, which frames the ridge on its westerly side, is a well-watered, well-tilled garden which the mountain traveler never tires of gazing down upon. Climbing the higher peaks from this valley floor, he may leave behind the goldenrod and sumac of midsummer, encounter a profusion of earlier months' flowers on the way up, and find violets in bloom at the highest levels. Situated low in the temperate zone, the Park area is the meeting-ground of plant-life of the north and south, and altitude gives these a succession of constant bloom.

Lateral spurs from the main ridge, like close-knit vertebrae in a giant's backbone, vary the width of the Park from 5 to 15 miles. Its boundaries wind through the foothills, enclosing roughly 327,000 acres of magnificent mountainous country. Within this area are piled twenty peaks over 3,500 and two over 4,000 feet high, separated by deep, wild ravines heavily wooded with virgin timber. A recurring ledge or shoulder along the eastern side of the central ridge gives rise to a line of steep, rocky cliffs from which one looks down over the tops of giant hemlocks, oaks, and black birches into the ever-changing valley of the Shenandoah. Along these escarpments are hidden glens so deeply shaded that the growth of moss and fern is almost subtropical in its luxuriance. In a more romantic age, a whole library of "Grimm's Fairy Tales" could be conjured up in these dim forest glades, where a hundred fairylands spur the explorer's imagination.

The inner valleys between the great ridge and its spurs form a world apart. Many of these are so inaccessible from the outside that they have been little visited, and lumbering in them is impossible. Cliffs worn by water-courses make veritable canyons of many of these valleys, where large streams, such as the Hughes River, Hazel River, Hawksbill Creek, Devil's Staircase Run, the renowned Rapidan, and scores of others, originate. Notable among these is White Oak Canyon, a narrow, precipitous defile filled with virgin timber of surprising variety down which an unnumbered series of waterfalls carries the rushing stream to a depth of 2,500 feet into the Piedmont Plain, in a length of 4 miles. Kettle Canyon, typical of a hundred ravines down which leaping streams rush into the South Branch of the Shenandoah, earns its name from the witch's brew of mist which it distils in mysterious fashion even in clear weather. Little wonder, perhaps, that in midsummer, ice crystals may be found below the packed leaves at its bottom, where huge boulders are tumbled like a Titan's toys and the sun's rays never penetrate. The Rapidan rises in a dense rhododendron thicket a mile in extent, to flow down a richly wooded ravine between Fork and Doubletop Mountains. The beauties of this section make it certain that it was not for the fishing alone that President Hoover, lover of the outdoors, pitched his summer camp here.

While the whole Park is a panorama of wild and beautiful scenery, its crowning glory is its waterfalls. Its streams have literally never been counted, some not even named; a hundred such, large and small, take their foaming courses into the eastern or western plain, down gorges consisting of a succession of falls of the greatest beauty and diversity. To climb any one of these canyons from the bottom, ascending between fern-hung cliffs from trout-pool to cascade, from tumbling rapids to waterfall, at once translates the explorer from the world of whirring wheels into the forgotten realm of the moccasin. It must have been in such mountain fastnesses that Indians bade their last defiance to advancing civilization; strangely enough, it is to these same retreats that the conquering white now betakes himself for surcease from its pressure.

A rendezvous of hawks, fierce bandits of the air, the weather-graven profile of the old man of the mountain maintains its age-long vigil over the winding Shenandoah, 3,000 feet below, across the twin ridges of the Massanutten Mountains, and, beyond the broad North Shenandoah Valley, over three ridges of the Alleghanies, far away in West Virginia. Could he turn his craggy head, he could note by night the moving finger of the Anacostia airplane beacon, an even hundred miles to the west by the highway.

To be at the crest of this peak in brilliant sunshine affects the observer like a strain from the National Anthem. The landscape change from the placidity of a painting by Charlotte Coman into the dramatic aspect of one by Doré. Thunderstorms march along the valley like invading armies, with flashes of artillery and rumbles of cannonade, observed from 20 miles away.

Hawksbill, Fork Mountain, Hog Back, Marshall, Mary's Rock, Bear Fence Mountain, Black Rock, and as many others, afford different outlooks, each as arresting. The already completed section of the Appalachian Trail through this region makes all of these viewpoints accessible to the mountain-lover afoot. The finest view of the range itself is obtained from Ragged Mountain, lovingly known among natives as "Old Rag," a peak with the individuality of a stark, jagged summit, standing off from the east front of the chain like a reviewing general. From the strangely balanced rock masses at its crest, the magnificent panorama of the whole region is a memorable sight.

The Shenandoah National Park, although utterly dissimilar to any of the western parks, has at once a charm and a grandeur which are its own. In spring, its rich vegetation fills it with a wild and tender charm, and the preponderance of deciduous trees makes the end of its summer a glorious carnival of color. It is then that the summits of its mountains, veiled in the faint haze that gives the ridge its name, seem a perfect setting to those lines of brooding beauty:

Brown-haired Autumn, silent maid,
Who, in her hood of haze,
Sat pensive on the far blue hills,
And watched, with dreamy eyes, the fading year.

Club Activities

PATC hikers in southern Pennsylvania, 1930's

Club Planning Social Program

October 1932

The Trail Club has long contemplated the launching of a building program to extend its hut and shelter system but has not considered it advisable to undertake this work until a way was seen to finance the project. Some of our members have suggested the idea of planning a few indoor social events (dances and card parties) during the winter and using the proceeds to build up a Shelter Fund. The President of the Club has appointed a committee to make arrangements for one of these parties early in the fall, and you will likely hear from this committee very soon. We hope that all members will cooperate heartily in this plan and that by the time of our next Annual Meeting we may have the nucleus of a fund that will assure the construction of shelters at points on the Trail where they are much needed.

Trail Club Activities

Paper read by H. C. Anderson before Southern Virginia Trail
Conference, October 29, 1932
From the Bulletin of January 1933

The first program of work to which the Potomac Appalachian Trail Club turned its attention was the scouting, clearing, and marking of a section of the Appalachian Trail. As the magnitude of the task unfolded before us, we saw the necessity of interesting as many workers as possible and of getting money with which to purchase tools and meet the other expenses of the Club work. This meant a campaign of publicity and education with a view of getting new members and telling people generally about the Appalachian Trail movement. Although the movement had then been under way for a number of years, it was surprising to find a general ignorance of what it was all about. To many it signified a motor route, because of the unfortunate and unwarranted application that has been made of the word "trail" to automobile roads. I remember interviewing one man, a retired physician, who owned some land along the route of our trail. After explaining to him at considerable length the idea and purpose of the Appalachian Trail I was somewhat nonplussed at the question, "Do you intend to pave your trail before you finish it?"

Thus it was that at an early stage of the development of our Club we came to a realization that a program of education was quite as important a part of our activities as the physical work of constructing and maintaining the trail. After all, no matter how beautiful trails we may build, if they are not used as intended our efforts will have failed their purpose. Our program of education consisted, first, in the writing of articles for outdoor magazines and distributing the reprints thereof, and in getting such publicity as we could in the Washington and Baltimore newspapers. Later on, we found that the newspapers of the towns near the route of the trail were only too glad to give space to matter telling about the Appalachian Trail, and these newspapers have been the medium of a great deal of trail publicity. Then we began to hold meetings with illustrated lectures on outdoor subjects. We soon found that an effective way of telling our story was by means of pictures, and the photographing of views from points along the trail was encouraged by photographic contests, the prizes being awarded at meetings especially held for that purpose, at which the more meritorious pictures were exhibited. Slides were made of quite a large number of the pictures, which became the property of the Club. Some of our members possessed themselves of movie cameras, and the Club has gradually acquired a collection of moving picture films showing not only views from the trail but trail clearing and other Club activities.

As our section of the trail neared completion the necessity of a guidebook became apparent. Our first edition of the *Guide to Paths in the Blue Ridge*, consisting of 500 copies, was published in December 1931, and this edition has now been practically exhausted. The guidebook has had many favorable reviews and has been sold in all parts of the East and also in the Middle West. It has been an instrument of considerable publicity for the Appalachian Trail.

Booklets on trail construction and maintenance and on hiking and camping equipment have also helped to spread the gospel of the out-of-doors. The Club Bulletins have contained not only announcements of the Club's activities but also information concerning the trail and the progress of the Appalachian Trail movement. These bulletins have been the means of interesting many in the Appalachian Trail, as well as in our own Club. Window displays have been made as a graphic representation of Trail Club activities. At the present time, we have four windows of the Washington office of the American Automobile Association devoted to displays of hiking and camping equipment and supplies, trail-clearing tools, trail signs and markers, Club publications, maps and photographs, all clearly designated by placards.

The importance of educational activities cannot be too strongly emphasized. The completion of the physical construction of the trail is now in sight, but our work is only just begun. At the present time those who are really interested in such a project as the Appalachian Trail constitute an insignificant portion of our country's population. If the Appalachian Trail is to be a permanent thing, we shall have to interest much larger numbers in hiking, camping, and allied outdoor activities.

We need also to get across to people the idea of the plan and purpose of the Appalachian Trail, but we want to be sure that we ourselves have grasped it with all its implications.

The Appalachian Trail is, so far as possible, a wilderness footpath, and hence requires a primeval environment. We are accused of selfishness in seeking to preserve the primeval condition of the more or less narrow strip of mountainous country through which our trail passes. If it were made more accessible by automobile roads scaling its heights and permeating its depths, hundreds of thousands more could enjoy the scenic beauties of this region which we would have restricted to a limited few. The answer is that the numbers who can enjoy a primeval environment are necessarily limited. The great mass of people probably do not have the capacity to enjoy a primeval environment. If hordes are thrown into a primeval environment, it soon disappears. It is possible to reach a saturation point. Therefore, our trail should not be made too accessible.

An illustration of the saturation point as applied to the new Skyline Drive in the Shenandoah National Park was afforded last Sunday. This road had been opened to the public only the day before. I happened to be at the entrance of the road in Thornton Gap at about four o'clock Sunday afternoon. A long line of cars extending out of sight stood waiting to get into the new road. A friend remarked that the attraction of the road was gone under such conditions. It was too much like driving along F Street. It remains to be seen what the congestion of the road will be after the novelty has worn off, but this proposition seems fairly obvious: The enjoyment of scenery per person will be in inverse ratio to the number of cars on the road. Note that I have said scenery enjoyment, for there is a class of people in whom the gregarious instinct is so strong that they seem to get the greatest enjoyment in being where there is a large crowd. But it is clear that if you are driving in a procession along a mountain road, with cars passing you from the opposite direction, your ability to absorb the scenery, however wonderful it may be, is very much restricted.

It is likewise possible for the saturation point to be reached on sections of the Appalachian Trail. If certain sections of the trail are made so accessible that on Sundays they are filled with picnic parties, we no longer have a primeval environment.

Let us clearly face the issue. Admitting that the use of our remnants of the primeval environment must of necessity be somewhat limited, is it worthwhile preserving? Most of us have a profound conviction that it is. The blind forces of a machine age would destroy what there is left to us of our primeval heritage. We should therefore strive by individual and group activity to get our message across before it is too late.

An essential to the success of a trail club is to get as many people at work as possible. In the early stages of an organization such as ours, a limited few usually carry the burden of most of the work. But if a trail club is to hold the interest of its members, it must give as many of them as possible a specific thing to do. This has been brought about in our organization by appointing trip leaders outside the officers as far as possible, and by means of committees. The burden of planning the Club trips and seeing that they were successfully carried out was put in the hands of an excursions committee. Another committee was appointed to take care of the publicity and educational work. Committees on guidebook, shelters, equipment and tools, signs, photographs, and maps, indicate the extent to which it has been possible to distribute the responsibility of the Club's work. The Supervisor of Trails has distributed the responsibility for the maintenance of the trail by appointing trail overseers. In the hands of each has been placed a section of the trail short enough in length for him to see that it is kept properly maintained without too burdensome an effort. The responsibility for the Club Bulletins has been placed in the hands of an editor. And so we have endeavored as far as possible to get the rank and file of our members at work in one capacity or another.

And now I come to what is perhaps the most important phase of our subject. You have seen the diversity of work that may be done by a trail club, but the primary purpose of a trail club should be recreation. However altruistic may be the avowed purpose of a trail club, the recreational should predominate its activities. When we speak of spreading the gospel of the out-of-doors, we should never get the idea that we are in any sense reformers or evangelists sacrificing ourselves to make the world better. A trail club is, above all things, a group of people banded together for the purpose of enjoying a certain form of outdoor recreation, and the activities of the Club should be planned with the view of affording the members the recreation they need and have a right to expect. Trips should regularly be scheduled purely for the purpose of recreation. The Club Bulletins should not be confined to utilitarian matter such as announcements of trips, technical information concerning the trail, equipment, and such matters, but there should also be a place therein for matter of a personal, humorous, or literary nature. Campfire singing and story telling should be encouraged. Other activities of a recreational nature will suggest themselves as the Club develops.

What I have called work should be done not as work but as play. The distinction between work and play is very clearly brought out by Benton MacKaye in his book "The New Exploration."

He first recounts one of the adventures of Tom Sawyer:

"Tom dwells with his Aunt Polly. Their home is in a little Missouri town on the banks of the Mississippi River. Tom returns home on Friday night covered with mud. For this crime, he is sentenced by Aunt Polly to hard labor on the following day (Saturday) while the other children will be at play. The sentence consists in whitewashing the long, high, front fence. The Saturday sun rises on a beautiful spring morning. Tom appears at the end of the fence, bucket and brush in hand. He starts to work. He daubs the brush along the first board and then stops to survey the 'far-reaching continent of unwhitewashed fence.' He sits down discouraged. The long, blank fence spells for him a virtually endless period of blank toil. Then he hears the merry voices of his schoolmates, released for a day of play. They are coming his way. His troubles forthwith double. Added to the despair of slavery is the rending terror of his disgrace. The world turns black. At this dark moment Tom is seized with an inspiration, 'nothing less than a great, magnificent inspiration.' He picks up his brush and goes 'tranquilly to work.' Along comes Ben Rogers, the very boy, of all the boys, whose ridicule Tom had most dreaded. He takes in Tom's situation at a glance, or thinks he does. 'Hello, old chap, you got to work, hey?' Tom keeps on painting. Ben again reminds Tom of his disgrace. Tom steps back. He surveys his work 'with the eye of an artist.' He makes another pass or two and then squints again. Ben becomes interested. 'Say, Tom, let me paint a little.' But Tom will not listen. Ben presses his case; he offers first the core of the apple he is eating, and finally the whole fruit, for the chance to take a hand. Tom ultimately relents. Other boys come and the process is repeated. They come to jeer but remain to whitewash. At the end of the day, the fence has been painted and Tom finds himself rich in the local juvenile currency of apple cores, broken pen-knives, crippled cats, and other forms of junk, all obtained as the price of whitewashing privileges. And Tom, in pondering upon the events of the day, discovers a great truth. It can be told in two sentences as follows: Work is what you are obliged to do. Play is what you are not obliged to do.

An illustration of how hard physical work may be done in the spirit of play is our trail-cleaning trips. Prior to this year our trail work was all done by informally arranged parties of limited numbers. Those that went on these trips enjoyed them more than the scheduled hiking trips. Other members expressed the desire to go on work trips, and it was finally decided to schedule a work trip open to the members as a whole. Larger numbers, of both sexes, turned out for this trip than for the hiking trips. They worked like beavers. And though with many the day ended with aching muscles, blistered hands, scratched arms, and bodies soaked and chilled by the rain, all insisted that they had had a bully time. Now our work trips are more popular than the other trips.

To recapitulate:

1. While the most obvious activity of a trail club is to construct and maintain trails, for a trail club interested in the Appalachian Trail, a no less important activity is a program of education. A trail, to be of value, must be used. Furthermore, if we are to preserve the primeval environment, which is an essential feature of the Appalachian Trail, increasing numbers must be interested in the form of outdoor recreation for which we stand.

2. An important principle in planning the activities of a trail club is to divide the work and distribute the responsibility as far as possible.

If this is done, the activities may be expanded, and interest and enthusiasm will be increased.

3. The recreational should predominate the club's activities. If we do not take the play attitude toward our club's activities, we have not entered into the spirit of the Appalachian Trail idea.

Truck Trail Traverse

by David J. Guy
November 1946

The "Truck Trail Traverse," the TTT series for short, will be initiated November 16 at Rockfish Gap, Va. This will mark the beginning of a 267-mile hike to the Susquehanna River above Harrisburg, Pa. A large number of aspirants are expected, at least for the initial occasion. Some will hike all the way, some will hike just what they can and ride in between, and still others who find it impossible to go on all trips of the series are welcome to go when the dates are suitable. Here is offered an opportunity for Club members to see the less frequented parts of the Potomac Section of the famous Maine-to-Georgia Appalachian Trail.

For the initial November trip, Henry B. George will be leader. The plan is as follows: the party will travel via the Deluxe Truck and some private cars to an attractive tourist camp near Swift Run Gap; there to lodge Friday and Saturday nights. The proprietor of the camp will buy, cook, and serve the food using the Club's camping equipment. Cabins have electric lights and running water but no heat, so bring sleeping bag or an extra blanket. A large heated cottage will serve as a dining room.

The first leg of the TTT series will be hiked Saturday, November 16, over open-topped mountains with superb panoramic views immediately north of Rockfish Gap. The hiking distance will be about 11 miles, after which the party will return to the tourist camp at Swift Run Gap. The second leg will be hiked Sunday, November 17, ending at the Doyle River Shelter, hiking distance about 14 miles. The truck will shuttle between camp and Trail, and Sunday dinner will be had at camp. The party will leave Club Headquarters Friday evening and return late Sunday evening. Total cost, $11. Watch for the reservation notice.

The third and fourth legs of the traverse will be hiked December 7 and 8, with the same tourist camp as a base. Jack Hess will be leader. The TTT series is not a marathon; distances are moderate and gauged by the amount of climbing required. On these first two trips there will be time to enjoy the beauty of mountains and valleys, the deep hollows and sharp ridges, to see their naked shapes, for the leaves will be down come late autumn. And there will be fellowship, tall stories, good food, and "harmonee-ee."

Omitting the cold months of January and February and the hot months of July and August, the plan is to complete the traverse in two years. A tentative schedule follows:

1   Rockfish Gap to Turk Gap crossing, 11 miles, November 16, 1946*
2   Turk Gap to Doyle River Shelter, 14 miles, November 17, 1946*
3   Doyle River Shelter to Powell Gap, 12 miles, December 7. 1946*
4   Powell Gap to Pocosin Shelter, 13 miles, December 8, 1946*
5   Pocosin Shelter to Spitler Knoll Overlook, 13 miles, March 1947
6   Spitler Knoll Overlook to Thornton Gap, 15 miles, April 1947
7   Thornton Gap to Little Hogback Mountain crossing, 13 miles, May 1947
8   Little Hogback to Chester Gap, 13 miles, June 1947
9   Chester Gap to Rock Spring, 14 miles, September 1947
10 Rock Spring to near Snickers Gap, 14 miles, October 1947
11 Near Snickers Gap to Keys Gap, 14 miles, November 1947
12 Keys Gap to Crampton Gap, 14 miles, December 1947
13 Crampton Gap to Black Rock--Bagtown Road, 14 miles, March 1948
14 Bagtown Road to Pen Mar, 14 miles, April 1948
15 Pen Mar to Mt. Alto-Sanatorium Road, 12 miles, May 1948
16 Sanatorium Road to Ridge Road near Milesburn Shelter, 13 miles, June 1948
17 Milesburn Shelter to Tag Run Lean-to, 16 miles, September 1948*
18 Tag Run Lean-to to Brantsville, 14 miles, September 1948*
19 Brantsville to U. S. Route 11, 10 miles, October, 1948*
20 U. S. Route 11 to Susquehanna River, 11 miles, October 1948*

*Two day trips

Skylarking at Skyland
July 16-17, 1932

by Otis H. Gates

The annual midsummer frolic of the Club at Skyland, Va., tallying each year of the organization's existence, has become a habit, a tradition, an institution, like the depression, or hay fever, or the income tax. This year the time chosen for the event was the weekend of July 16-17.

So it came to pass that on a Saturday in July the caravan of the faithful and their guests set out on the fourth annual pilgrimage to Mecca-on-the-Trail. Thirty of the party let Hutchison do it and journeyed in the coach; while those who rolled their own, with their passengers, numbered twenty-two.

The coach party, disembarking at the foot of the mountain, made the ascent on foot in a leisurely and straggling fashion, pausing to browse on the roadside blueberries or to enjoy the views at the various vantage points. Overtaking them at intervals came the cars, conveying those making the trip in that manner. As the coach-and-foot party attained the top and emerged from the wooded road, the waning daylight was suddenly and prematurely extinguished by the shadow of the canopy of mist clouds now close overhead, the effect being the darkness of nightfall. But simultaneously the beckoning lights of Skyland burst brightly into view only a few rods ahead, and these late comers quickly joined the earlier arrivers already congregated at dinner.

Later in the evening there was, of course, the dance with carnival decorations and atmosphere. This was followed, in the wee, small hours of the morning, by a rousing bonfire. In the forenoon, a number of hikes were taken. One group went to Miller's Head; another chose the Passamaquoddy Trail and Stony Man; while White Oak Canyon, with its friendly shade, rugged cliffs, leaping cataracts, and especially the swimming pool, attracted the most part.

Dinner was served at 2:30. Feasting, however, was only one of

Facing camera from left: Jow Winn, Bill Mersch, driver, 1936

the features of that elaborate, animated, colorful, and soundful affair. What with the general impromptu dancing and parading between the courses, the continuous efforts of the musicians, the confused sounds of the prevailing exuberant gaiety, the carnival effects in the form of fantastic and gaudy headdress, confetti ribbons unreeling overhead and entwining the dancers and strewing the floor, and vari-colored balloons bobbing about, the gala celebration may not inappropriately be described as a cross between a night club and a national political convention. Who is he of serious men who now commands silence that he may be heard to read from parchment scroll? A plague on the fellow! On with the dance! Let joy be unconfined! But look! 'Tis the royal Harold from the court of "Myronides the First, Emperor of Appalachia," who reads. And hark! He reads a proclamation given under the king's hand and seal, commemorating and celebrating the name and fame of a valiant knight for his feat in transporting, singlehanded and scornful of proferred assistance, two hefty, bulky, and cumbersome posts to the summit of Mary's Rock. These posts, originally intended merely to serve the prosaic, utilitarian purpose of supports for trail signs, are, by virtue of the royal ukase, ordained and dedicated as pillars of the Club's Hercules and a perpetual double memorial and monument to a rare and happy combination of, to quote the regal tribute, "a strong back and a weak mind." Thus, for two hours the party feasted and disported itself, a fitting culmination of a day and a half replete with pleasure and recreation, and then into the cars, or down the mountain on foot to the coach, and homeward.

The Trilliam Trip
Chester Gap to Ashby Gap
May 13, 1934

Meeting the demand for a trip through the section between Manassas and Ashby Gaps during the season when wild flowers are in bloom, an old favorite has been rescheduled. The trip has been arranged to offer two alternatives. The long trip will be a distance of 17 miles from Chester Gap to Linden and then to Ashby Gap. The shorter trip, a distance of 10 miles, will be from the foot of the mountain in Manassas Gap through to Ashby Gap. After dropping the party for the long hike at Chester Gap, the bus will carry the remainder of the party to Manassas Cap for the 10-mile trip. This short trip is the same as that taken last year but in the reverse direction. The Trail itself leads through a very pleasing forest growth. However, it is the profusion of bloodroot, violets, and trilliums that makes this an unforgettable trip. The panoramic views on the north, and particularly from Signal Knob, are extremely fine. (On the east slope from Signal Knob is a Civil War cemetery.)

Historic Trails
June 8, 9, and 10, 1934

Turning from the usual practice of opening trails, the Club will on this trip follow some of the trails opened at the very beginning of American history. We will retrace the routes followed by Washington in his campaigns against the French, by Braddock when he marched from the Coast to attack Fort Duquesne, and by Washington when he went to the Ohio country just before and just after the close of the Revolutionary War.

By careful research these routes have all been worked out. The

plan is to have a two-and-a-half day trip following the line of Braddock's march almost to the battlefield, and on the return, swinging
into West Virginia, crossing the ranges of the Alleghenies, and following the trails of Washington.

This trip is primarily a bus trip, with only short walks to points of
scenic and historic interest along the way. This type of trip is distinctly novel in the Club program and will no doubt be of considerable
interest to those who do not always find it practicable to participate in
the usual walks. The historic aspects have been very fully developed,
but apart from this, the trip offers an opportunity to see some of the
striking scenery of the Allegheny Mountains and western Pennsylvania, Maryland, and West Virginia.

The bus will leave Washington at 2 p.m. Friday, June 8; Friday
night will be spent in Cumberland and Saturday night in Morgantown,
West Virginia. The bus will reach Washington late Sunday evening,
June 10.

The total distance will be approximately 600 miles. In general, the
route will go through Snickers Gap, Martinsburg, Hancock,
Cumberland, Uniontown, to Mount Pleasant, and on the return, south
to Morgantown on the Monongahela, Fairmont, Grafton, Romney,
and Winchester.

Among the places of interest covered by this trip are Cumberland,
the head of the old Chesapeake and Ohio Canal, looking up The Nar-
rows, Town Hill, Great Meadows, Fort Necessity, Braddock's Grave,
and the locale of many interesting incidents of Indian and frontier
history in the valleys of what is now West Virginia. It will cross Sideling
Hill, Town Hill, Green Ridge, Polish Mountain, Martin Mountain,
Big Savage, Meadow Mountain, Keyser's Ridge (the highest point
on the National Trail east of the Rockies), the Youghiogheny, Tygert's
Valley, Cheat Mountain and the Cheat River, North Branch of the
Potomac Valley, Pattersons Creek, South Branch Valley, the great
North Mountain, and the Shenandoah Valley.

For an account of these trails, see "The Travels of George Washington," by W. J. Showalter, in *National Geographic Magazine*, January, 1932; *Historic Highways of America*, by Archer B. Hulbert, Vols.
2 and 3; *George Washington Diaries*, edited by John C. Fitzpatrick;
and the *West Virginia Historical Magazine,* Vol. II, No. 3, Page 31.

Nicholson Hollow Folks, 1932

Marys Rock to Nethers
September 16, 1934

This trip will take the Club over a portion of the new trail recently constructed for the Club by the CCC to replace the old Appalachian Trail which was taken for the Skyline Drive. The way will be south from Panorama, affording an outlook over Hazel Hollow, and thence over the always delightful Marys Rock (3,514 feet) to the Pinnacle (3,720 feet), where views may be had in all directions. We will then turn aside from the Trail to Sexton Shelter, the probable stopping point for lunch.

Leaving Sexton Shelter, we will continue along the Appalachian Trail to the head of Free State (Nicholson) Hollow. From this point, we will follow the side trail down Free State Hollow, along Hughes River, to Nethers. Most of the way down this hollow, the trail follows an old road which, from time to time, passes mountain cabins. This hollow has a particularly interesting background, as in the past it was the home territory of one of the most turbulent mountain families and was a noted resort and refuge. The trip will offer the last opportunity Club members will have to see this section of the Blue Ridge still occupied by its native inhabitants. The total distance will be approximately 13 miles.

Joint Trail Clubs Hike
From Supervisor's Comments
July 1935

In anticipation of the joint hike of the Pennsylvania, Maryland, and District of Columbia clubs, the Baltimore group went over the North Mountain section for which they provide overseers, cleared and painted it. The week following the hike, they relocated the Trail at Overview, overlooking the Susquehanna River, eliminating several complicated turns and badly cut-up roads. While I did not have the pleasure of going on the joint trip, I have heard from all sides good reports of the condition of the Trail and of the interest taken in the trip by Scott Burgoon, George Spangler, and other Boy Scout leaders who are assisting the Baltimore group in maintaining the sections. The Washington group returned singing praises of the hospitality of the Pennsylvanians, and the pleasant contacts made there will be long remembered. Certainly, if newspaper space is any indication, Harrisburg was thoroughly "Appalachian Trail conscious" before the weekend was over! Orville Crowder can well be pleased with the trip he planned and led. The interest created by it will certainly be reflected in the condition and use of the Trail on both sides of the Susquehanna River near Harrisburg in the future.

Maine Appalachian Trail Trip
August 24 to September 6, 1935

Full details of the P. AT C. trip over the 120 miles of Appalachian Trail from Monson to Katahdin are described in the mimeographed notice of this trip which has been mailed to Club members. The itinerary contemplates 13 days on the Trail in Maine. The walking distance averages slightly less than 10 miles; the shortest day's trip. The initial day is 6 miles, and the longest trip, over White Cap Mountain, is 15.5 miles. Two days of the program are devoted to lay-overs or side trips. One is to Joe Mary Mountain, or a canoe trip on the Joe Mary Lakes; the second is to "The Gulf" of Pleasant River. The cost from Monson to Millinocket for the entire trip is $55, exclusive of transportation to and from Washington.

Much interest has been manifested in the trip and, to provide better accommodations, it may be necessary to divide the party into two sections, one following the other at an interval of a day's journey. Two days will be spent at Katahdin, the culminating point of the entire trip.

For uniqueness of travel through an absolute wilderness with comfortable accommodations at low cost over a well-marked and maintained trail, this excursion will provide a most unusual experience to the Club members who are fortunate enough to participate. Additional copies of the detailed announcement and itinerary of the trip may be obtained from Assistant Secretary Fulkerson.

The Catoctins
September 22, 1935

The first Club trip to the Catoctin Range, which we have crossed many times en route to the Blue Ridge, is now scheduled. Although lower in height, the Catoctins are of much interest. Their waterfalls and streams are outstanding. Much of the area is a public preserve, for mining a part of the watershed of the City of Frederick. This is the region where the Supervisor of Trails has been threatening, for some time, to establish an elaborate side trail system in the Club's leisure, if that state ever arrives. This will be the Club's initial excursion to the section to see, at first hand, if it is all that the reports have indicated. At the present time, the exact route of the trip is being developed. The features will be announced by the postcard reminder.

Tri-Club Trip
Swift Run Gap to Rockfish Gap
October 24-25, 1936

This is a repetition of the marathon of some two years ago, "where the wind blew away a mile of the trail on Ivy Creek," the 60-mile hurricane and other legends, which have furnished material for many a campfire story. The 1936 version of this trip, for the most part, will be over the new Park Service graded trail as far as Jarman Gap. The old route, it will be recalled, because of the difficulties of developing an amateur trail along the ridge crest from Black Rock to the south, followed the North and South Forks of Moormans River: High Top, Black Rock, and many peaks unknown to us as yet afford unusual views.

This trip will give an opportunity to become familiar with an entirely new section of the Shenandoah Park. The marathon is also an occasion for the anticipated annual excursion with our neighbors to the south, the Natural Bridge Appalachian Trail Club and the Roanoke Appalachian Trail Club. The Clubs will meet Saturday evening and join in the hike on the second day. The return from Rockfish Gap will be made late Sunday evening. Bus will leave Washington Friday night and that night will be spent at the Spotswood Tavern at Elkton. The

PATC hikers crossing the Shenandoah River by ferry at Harper's Ferry, October 1940

hike each day will be about 21 miles.

For map, see PATC Trail Map of Shenandoah National Park (Southern Section) and U. S. G. S. Map of Shenandoah National Park (south half); the new trail route does not appear on either map

At the end of the first day's trip, the bus will take the party to the rendezvous with the other Trail Clubs. Accommodations may be somewhat crowded and participants on the trip must be prepared accordingly.

A Trail Club Songbook

July 1932

Several months ago, the Council authorized P. L. Ricker and J. F. Schairer to form a committee for preparing a Club songbook. For this purpose, 105 songs, including 5 Club prize contest songs, have been selected. It is expected that the book will be ready for the White Mountain trip, with possible proofs for the Skyland Frolic. You who are interested in singing, or who can even make a joyful noise, and would like to meet occasionally to learn the music of the new Club songs, please send your name and address to P. L. Ricker.

Club Songbook to be Issued Soon
July 1933

At a recent Council Meeting of the Club, Chairman P. H. Ricker of the Songbook Committee announced that the collection of songs adopted for use by the Club would soon be ready to present to members in book form. That will solve the difficulty of finding songs that everyone knows, when, around the campfire and elsewhere, we get the urge to raise our voices in tuneful melody.

Our Club Song

We are presenting the beautiful and inspiring words of our official Club song in the hope that members will familliarize themselves with the lines so that our song leader can have more enthusiastic support in our occasional ensemble singing. Unfortunately, the Club songbook has not yet become a fact, and we cannot provide the music here, but you cannot help learning the tuneful melody if you come along on some of the Club trips and join in when Joe Winn directs our impromptu vocal efforts.

The Appalachian Trail

by Helen Stone and Edna L. Stone
Copyright 1931, Published October 1933

From Mount Katahdin's summit high
To slopes of southern pine,
The long brown path is winding
Its way near timberline.
O'er wild and rocky uplands
It leads us sure and true,
With only winds of heaven
Between us and the blue.

Chorus
Oh! Some may yearn for the salty sea,
And some for speed may long,
But I'll adventure in Arcady
Where the long brown path leads on!
Oh! Let my feet forever seek,
While strength is firm and hale,
The uplands high, against the sky,
On the Appalachian Trail!

The long brown path is turning
From hill to forest way;
It seeks the fern-clad woodland
Where falling waters play;
It brings us to the campfire,
To food and blissful rest,
To Friendship's hearty welcome,
True answer to our Quest.

Repeat Chorus

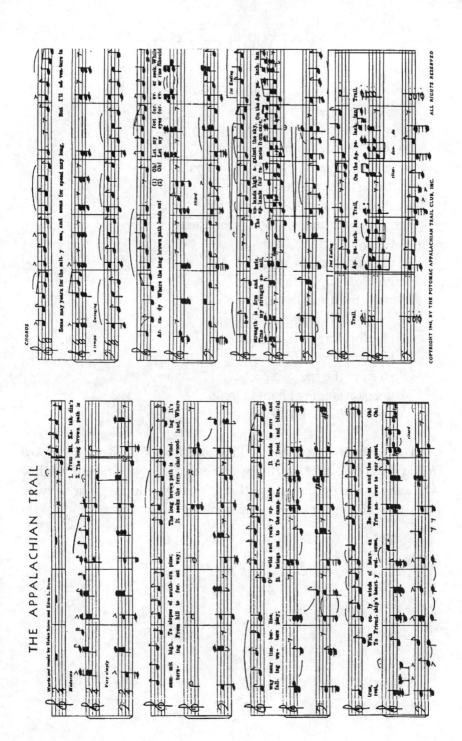

THE APPALACHIAN TRAIL

Trail Worker's Song

October 1944

We clip, and weed, and chop, and paint
On the Trail the whole day through,
For clip, and weed, and chop, and paint
Are things we like to do.
We throw out sticks, and logs, and briars,
And cook our lunches over camp fires,
On the Trail, on the Trail,
On the Appalachian Trail,
Heigh-Ho, Heigh-Ho,
To make our troubles go,
We clear the Trail and sing all day,
Heigh-Ho, Heigh-Ho, Heigh-Ho,
Heigh-Ho, Heigh-Ho,
When from the trail we go,
We keep on singing all night long
With a Heigh, Heigh-Ho!

These words, sung to the familiar tune from Walt Disney's "Snow White and the Seven Dwarfs," were composed by Elizabeth Aughey while she was working on the Ridge Trail on Old Rag. On the way home, she taught the song to the truckload of workers.

A Word About Tin Cans

October 1932

The comments of a nonmember on the Trail Club's "tincan activities" have led one of our very active members, Mr. Neil E. Stevens, to bring to our attention a practice which in no way adds to the beauty of the Trail.

It seems that a goodly number of these discarded food receptacles have accumulated around Sexton and Meadow Springs shelters. It is true that some of these may have been left by outsiders and not by Club members; but it is also true that most of us have seen some of this promiscuous tin can throwing. Even if we have not ourselves been guilty, Mr. Stevens comments, "No doubt a good bit of this tin can throwing is excused by the throwee on the grounds that there are no mosquitoes in the Appalachians. This is in a measure true, but in a few places where there is stagnant water, mosquitoes do occur. I will risk a bet of anything portable I own except my dugout canoe that if we keep on throwing tin cans for five years longer, we can introduce mosquitoes in at least a dozen places on our Trail. This would be a grand entomological experiment and a valuable object lesson."

How about it, Trailers? Can't we find some better way of disposing of our lunch rubbish than leaving the containers of our favorite brand of canned hash or pork and beans cans to decorate the landscape? We ask your help in an "Anti-Tin Can Campaign."

How We Came to Pick Apples

by H. C. Dickinson
October 1944

Early in the summer of last year, several members of the PATC remarked that it might be good fun and a useful service as well to pick apples in the fall for some of the owners of orchards along the Appalachian Trail who have been so cooperative in Trail matters. We have a lot of friends who have orchards with a lot of apples in them.

At a Council meeting, this question came up for discussion, and everyone thought it would be a good plan, so Bill Mersch was detailed to find out what could be done about it. Then regimentation raised its ugly head: wages are fixed. We could not pick apples for nothing, and we could not pick apples for less nor for more than the regulation wages. To do so might be taking away someone else's job. But the Trail Club members did not want to enter into wage competition with the boys and girls of the Shenandoah. In fact, they did not want wages, nor were they likely, so they thought, to be able to compete with the natives at so much per bushel. It looked very much as if wartime regulations, presumed to help get things done, would result in a lot of good apples rotting on the ground, although there were not enough natives to harvest the crop. Trail Club members should not get into the habit of going to the mountains and picking apples at starvation wages just to do the natives out of a job.

Thus, the project was stalled. But we found that owners of the orchards wanted help from any source they could find. At about the same time, someone had a new idea. Why not go by truck, as on other work trips, just for the fun of the trip, and the warm feeling of a job well done, each paying his own way, as always? Then the owners of the orchards could pay the Club whatever the law required them to pay. The Club has a good use for the proceeds. (They keep up headquarters; don't mention it.) Each worker was to get a half-bushel of apples free, and the privilege of buying more at a dollar a bushel, if he could find a place for them in the truck on the way home. This proved to be ample reward when added to the good time, good ride, good company, and generally, extra good weather.

Thus, the laws were satisfied, or evaded. The owners were satisfied, or said so. The Club members and some of their guests were satisfied, we know. The natives were satisfied, we hope. A few thousand bushels of apples ought to have been satisfied to be serving some useful purpose instead of rotting on the ground.

The 1943 season, which got a rather late start because of the legal complications, permitted four or five trips. Some private cars were enlisted to carry the overflows. The number of workers varied from 25 to 40. On the first trip, apples were picked from the trees with ladders, but for the most part they were "ground-hogged" off the ground. On one very busy day, 18 people gathered 800 bushels of apples. Whenever the homeward way led anywhere near Round Hill, Mrs. Ballenger of Corner Hall fed the crowd bountifully on fried chicken, with all the fixings, especially corn fritters. Then came frost and cold winter winds, and evenings before the fire to consume the apples we had brought home. One evening in particular will be long remembered, when all the apple pickers gathered together to celebrate.

The 1944 season, beginning early and with the same technique, promises six or eight sessions, some of which already have materialized. More than a thousand bushels of apples were gathered in one day by 36 people.

Camping Trips in Apple Orchards

by Madeline Haenny
October 1946

To some it may seem that there is quite a gulf between the primary objectives of the Club and working in apple orchards. And from a superficial point of view, it appears so.

We all know, however, that this work was started during the war years to help harvest the apple crop for several orchard owners over whose land our Trail passes. In 1943, 1944, and 1945, we picked a considerable quantity of apples when it was impossible to obtain the normal supply of labor. This year, we were again invited to help, and, so, the two-day apple-camping trips began.

Almost every Trail Club member knows the fun in a biking-camping trip. Well, apple-camping trips are also fun. At the present writing, our trips have been confined to the orchard of our good host, Charles W. Keyser, near Marshall, Virginia. Mr. Keyser chose a perfect camping spot for us in a grove of trees near the orchard. We have plenty of space for our "kitchen" and for our tents and a lovely vista down a fox-hunting trail. Our favorite perch is the stone fence from which we can view and smell the progress being made over the cooking fire; turn around and we have a splendid view of the mountains. Big and Little Cobblers are in the foreground. Behind them we can see Rattlesnake Mountain, The Peak, Compton Mountain, and Mt. Marshall. (Charlie Thomas says even Mary's Rock is visible on clear days.)

We learn about apples on these trips. This writer had never heard of apple-thinning. Personal experience had been had with carrots and beets, thinning, but apple-thinning, never. The results obtained are the same, a better and bigger product. To be able also, nonchalantly, to call an apple by its given name is an accomplishment, we think.

Ladder climbing isn't in quite the same category as mountain climbing. But there are few of us who have climbed mountains on an angle at which ladders are placed. If a ladder is almost perpendicular, however, seeming to rest on nothing but clouds, it is safe if "Goldie" says so. "Goldie" is the guardian of the orchard who looks after the ladies with great solicitude. He advocates "Safety First" always. If a ladder seems to be slipping precariously, one is to "make other arrangements immediately."

The popular spot after the day's work is over is the spring-fed pool, installed by Mr. Keyser primarily for storing water for spraying, but very much appreciated by us for swimming.

No account of a camping trip would be complete without mentioning the "eats." Imagine flapjacks with sausage and fried apples; sweet corn, green beans, and tomatoes fresh from the Coppage garden; T-bone steaks from Kennedy's store at Marshall; and of course, Charlie's incomparable coffee.

We get plenty of exercise, fresh air, sunshine, lovely mountain views, experience in camping technique, good fellowship, and fun on apple-camping trips.

Shelter Benefit Great Success

Anonymous
January 1937

Al Jackman and Frank Schairer (left to right), early 1930's

It was a grand party, that shelter benefit on February 17th. Though its main purpose may have been to raise revenue for equipping the numerous new shelters, Joe Winn's intention was evidently to give us all our money's worth, and that he did verily. Such a variety of entertainment, square dancing, cards, hospitality, but best of all, the floor show, and plenty of room for everything at Eastern High School! Joe not only outdid his reputation for uncovering the latent talents of his associates, but also proved beyond a shadow of a doubt that he is the "fellow with the magic brain and photographic mind."

The first skit with Orville Crowder and Joe Winn, dressed to the nines in top hats, tails, walking sticks and packs must have made even strangers hysterical. Orville's apparently endless supply of verses and the refrain, "Really?" "Yes." "Would you believe it?" should be preserved in print. The dance routine added the finishing touch. Joe says, "The act was to be a threesome, but Otis Gates was rendered *hors du combat* because of extensive excavations to his incisors, bicuspids and molars a week preceding the show."

Harold McCoy's recitations are always good, and "The Shooting of Dan McGrew" made an important contribution to the program.

Joe's mental magic was astounding! Interesting! Bewildering! The "Human Calendar," "The Lightning Calculator" and the "Man with the Photographic Mind" were all amazingly clever and required intense concentration, particularly difficult in the presence of a large audience.

"Our Nell," the mellerdrammer presented by our own PATC Barnstormers, was superb. The cast of characters was: the flint-hearted father, Franklin Durr; Little Nell, his daughter, George Clendaniel; a villain, Gordon Durr; the Constable, Harold Allen; Make-up specialist, Harold Allen. Can anybody ever forget George's lovely blonde curls and white satin dress supported by No. 12 shoes?

Orville's "Jumbled Facts" stunt was immensely entertaining and gave a great number of people opportunity to take part.

A Club party would not be complete without Joe's lightning cartoons. What a surprise to PATC evolve into Mickey Mouse on skis!

The closing moving picture reel showed among other things Scandinavian folk dancing, which led up to more square dancing called by Joe Winn to the accompaniment of our own PATC orchestra.

The various committee members contributed to the completeness of the affair by the resourceful dispatch of their duties. The entertainment was also a financial success, netting something like $140 for shelter equipment, maps, guidebook material and like "necessities."

Those who did not or could not attend really missed something!

Shelter Fund Entertainment a Success

Anonymous
July 1933

The Shelter Fund Entertainment held on April 18 at Pierce Hall proved a highly successful venture, resulting in a profit of $145. To E. Malcolm Wood and a large staff of very able assistants goes the credit for this achievement.

As a result of energetic salesmanship on the part of the Tickets Committee, especially Jewell Glass, Vivian Robb, Ken Boardman, and A. H. Jackman, we had present the record crowd of 280 members and friends who enjoyed the variety of entertainment offered.

Frank Schairer and Herman Nolte opened the show with a song which was written for the occasion. Then Joe Winn with his excellent chalk talk and "knight's march" effectively captured the interest. We had with us Benton McKaye, Nestor of the Appalachian Trail project, who made some interesting references to the beginnings of the Trail. Half an hour of Sylvia Meyer's delightful harp music passed all too quickly, after which Warner Tufts struck a responsive note in his readings. Then came the piece de resistance, in lighter vein. Dr. Schmeckebier, who had ably guided the course of the entertainment, was suddenly interrupted by the intrusion of the Inventor (Harold Allen), clad in a familiar garb. This unique character was full of ideas and labor-saving "inventions." After demonstrating the various clever devices he carried on his person, he called for his Traileomakus, which was slowly guided down the hall by its colorful crew, to the accompaniment of the jingle of the sleigh bells and the clanging of the gong. In the words of the Inventor, it was "unique! stupendous! sublime!" It was said to have everything except sex appeal, from a shelter snore harp (a device which some of us have had recent occasion to long for), Ouija Board "to tell if the rest of the party is lost," down to the veracity moonshine-testing compound, in fact everything necessary for a trip in the Blue Ridge.

The clever lines of this amusing skit were the joint work of Ken Boardman and Harold Allen, and to Tom Meyer, indeed to the entire

Meyer family, must go the credit for the actual construction of the Traileomakus, which is a distinct contribution, not only to our passing amusement, but also to the tradition of the Club. Much midnight oil was burned in the course of its construction and we would take this opportunity of expressing our appreciation for their help. To all those who assisted in any way to make the entertainment such a splendid success, the Club's thanks are due.

Country Dance and Entertainment

By Jeannette Speiden
July 1935

"Get your partners for the Virginia Reel! " Above the sound of many voices rose Joe Winn's commanding voice from the familiar megaphone. Bob Beach tuned his fiddle. Up and down the room the sets formed and soon eight "first ladies" were leading the Reel. The friends of dancing, who preferred to take time out for breath, were ranged along the wall having such a good time comparing notes on recent work trips that they had no eye for the amateurish efforts of the many who were attempting unfamiliar dances. Good old mountain dances! "Buffalo Gals," "The Lady of the Lake," "Nelly Bly!" Everyone enjoyed "Pop Goes the Weasel." Those who were accustomed to long days on the trail were still dancing when the time came for "The Lancers" and were intrepid enough to attempt its complex figures. When the dance ended they felt as though they had been hiking all day in a dense fog. It was real exercise but jolly good fun!

Joe Winn provided the program of entertainment in addition to acting as master of ceremonies and one-third of the orchestra. Wilman Spawn gave us a recitation dealing with a biological theme. Dr. L. H. Flint read some of his own poems. Harold McCoy was very convincing in the role of Kipling's Tommy Atkins. We hope that next year Joe Winn will start a drawing class and show some of the rest of us how to change a cow wearing a rosebud into a CCC boy (or a Trail Club member?) on a holiday. We hope that Joe will not, however, grow whiskers. We like to be able to see our Hillbilly Orchestra. If he ever grows whiskers, some of us will get out the pruning shears.

All of the one hundred and eighty-three members and friends who attended the party will agree that it was a success from every point of view. Those who had occasion to examine the state of the Treasury before and after the event found a difference of $101 in favor of the Club.

Thanks for the success of the party must be divided among many members who contributed both time and money. Jean Stephenson and Marion Park were on hand to make all the business arrangements and to make certain that everything ran smoothly. Joe, of course, was responsible for planning and carrying through the program. Many members of the Club purchased from three to five tickets. We can understand why some people consume two or three meals at the end of a day in the mountains, but the consumption of half a dozen dance tickets apiece is proof of a philanthropic spirit.

"On with the Dance!" The season for square dancing is over. All who have tried it agree that it is not a warm weather sport. But next year this part of the Club program will have instant and constant support from a large number of members.

Rock Climbing

October 1937

While the primary objective of the Potomac Appalachian Trail Club has been the maintenance of a section of the Appalachian Trail, and the trail program is still its principal objective, and probably its major appeal, the Club's activities are increasingly spreading into attendant fields. This is due, perhaps in part, to the development of the system and a very natural desire on the part of its members to undertake new fields of activity.

The latest phase which has attracted attention is rock climbing. The topographic conditions in this section afford little opportunity for the more technical phases of mountaineering. However, it is highly desirable that Club members should have an opportunity to become versed in this science, not only for its own value but for a fuller appreciation of the art of mountaineering.

So, making the best of its limited terrain, the Trail Club has undertaken a modest program on rock climbing. The newly formed Rock Climbing Committee is headed by James E. Lamb, Jr., 34 Knowles Avenue, Kensington, Maryland. Paul Bradt and Gustave A. Gambs are among its leading spirits. It is expected that the Committee will arrange instruction in rock climbing, schedule rock-climbing trips, and develop information on the available climbs in this vicinity. The Chairman will welcome suggestions for the development of this program. Anyone interested in rock climbing should send a card to Mr. Lamb.

Climber Ed Worrell rappelling

Rock-Climbing Trip to Bull Run Mountains

October 31, 1937

This will be the Club's first rock-climbing trip. It is to be a get-together party for climbers in this vicinity, giving them an opportunity to get acquainted with each other's favorite climbs and technique. This does not mean, however, that all those who go on this trip will be expected to participate in the rock-climbing.

The Bull Run Mountains will be remembered from the Mystery Trip of April, 1935, as an easily accessible and charming picnic spot. From the white quartzite cliffs are sweeping views westward across fields and woods with their autumn foliage. Those who wish to come only for the picnic and easy five-mile walk will be welcome. But they will have to entertain themselves, because the leader will be busy below hanging some of his friends on the rocks. You are even invited to come down and see how it is done.

Leader: Paul Bradt.

Cost and Directions: Bus fare and dinner, for member $1.85; for guest, $2.35. Bring lunch, canteen, cup, flashlight, change of footwear. Bus leaves Treasury Place at 7:00 a.m.

Skiing 1936

October 1937

The April 1936 *Bulletin* reported the extraordinary manifestation of the interest in skiing in Washington and indicated in a general way the program which the Club was adopting in connection with this latest outdoor activity. It is the feeling of the Club officers that the administration of the specialized features of skiing could be handled to better advantage by a group with skiing as its primary objective, but that the Club program should be adapted to provide for skiing and that there should be placed at the disposal of the Club membership the benefits which result from the size of the organization and its participation in outdoor activities. It seems that these benefits are two-fold.

First, arrangements should be made to have available locally suitable low-priced equipment which could be purchased by Trail Club members.

Second, arrangements should be made for a "dry course," or pre-season skiing instruction. Plans in both directions are being perfected. After extensive investigation, an inter-committee group from the Trail Club and the Washington Ski Club, consisting of W.W. Davies, Charles Smoot, and Harold Leich, have concluded that skiers in this region would be better served by having available the low-priced equipment issued by Ski Sport, Inc., 144 High Street, Boston. This equipment will be sold by the Sport Center, Eighth and D Streets, N.W. Trail Club and Ski Club members, on presentation of membership cards, will be entitled to a twenty percent discount from net prices. A circular is being sent to Trail Club members, listing a complete set of skiing equipment which should be satisfactory for conditions encountered in this region.

For its "dry course" instruction, the Club fortunately has been able to make arrangements whereby Douglas M. Burckett, Chairman of the Skiing Committee of the Appalachian Mountain Club, one of the outstanding authorities on skiing in New England, who conducts the dry courses for the Appalachian Mountain Club, will give similar instruction here on November 13 and 14. Admission to these courses will be on presentation of Club membership card only. Mountain Club of Maryland and Washington Ski Club members will also be admitted on presentation of their membership cards. Detailed information as to the dry course instruction and the standard recommended equipment is contained in the mimeographed circular which is being sent to Trail Club members.

The Excursions Committee will probably arrange its winter schedule so that when weather conditions permit, there will be an opportunity for skiing as well as for walking. Arrangements have also been made with the Park Service to clear an open slope free from rocks so that it may be used with a small amount of snowfall.

Skiing 1937

October 1937

Ski enthusiasts of the Club are making plans for an active season, despite an apparent lack of cooperation from the patron saint of skiers during the past winter. The dry course of pre-season skiing instruction, instituted in 1936 in cooperation with the Ski Club of Washington, will be continued this year. Four meetings have been planned to be held some time in November and December; further details will be announced later. Admittance will be granted only to members of the Trail Club, Ski Club, and Mountain Club of Maryland. Participants should bring old clothes and rubber-soled shoes. Locker rooms and showers will be available.

The Club is fortunate in being able to schedule ski trips with the knowledge that complete absence of snow does not mean that a trip is a total loss. Last winter, for example, the two scheduled skiing expeditions turned into orthodox hiking trips. The Committee is planning two more skiing and/or hiking trips, for the coming winter, and promises owners of fancy ash and hickory that sooner or later there will be skiing. A short section on winter sports equipment in the forth-coming edition of the Equipment List will provide information for those who wish to invest in winter-sports hardwood and hardware.

The skiing slopes cleared last autumn by the National Park Service and the CCC at Sexton Knoll and Rock Spring Shelter were used to advantage by Trail Club skiers on several occasions. A believe-it-or-not tale was brought back by one party that found excellent skiing at these slopes on Washington's Birthday, after a heavy thunderstorm on the night before. On the same day skiers in most of New England were sitting inside their hotels looking out at a rainstorm.

A recent scouting expedition to the grazing country west of Spruce Knob reported steep grassy slopes extending from 3500 feet to over 4000 feet, and rumors of 30-foot snowdrifts that sometimes last into June!

Additional Essays

*Mary Jo Williams, right, first editor of the PATC
Bulletin, 1932*

Sentinel of the Blue Ridge

by Myron Glaser
October 1952

Ragged Mountain, popularly known as "Old Rag", has come in for a lot of publicity lately. The imposing peak, a 3291-foot sentinel of the Blue Ridge Mountains of Virginia, has been described by Senator Harry F. Byrd of Virginia as his favorite spot for relaxation and meditation. In fact, he recently challenged his political adversary, Pickens Miller, to a climbing contest to its summit, an event he should surely win, for the Senator stated at the Pollock Knob Dedication October, 1951, that he had been up to Old Rag Summit twelve times during 1951. Senator Byrd is not the only prominent person to be encountered along Old Rag's craggy ridge. On a clear, crisp weekend, there is usually quite a bit of traffic over this challenging trail, for the mountain has, for over 25 years, been a favorite objective of the Potomac Appalachian Trail Club. Skyland guests were the first outlanders to find Old Rag. A horseback trail led down White Oak, around Robinson Mountain, through the town of Old Rag and part way up the mountain itself. A crude foot trail completed the journey to its gnarled and misshapen peak.

In 1928, Harold Anderson led one of the first expeditions to the fastnesses of the mountain. On that trip also were Frank Schairer, Stanley Searles, Tom Griffin, and myself. After study of the available maps, it was decided that the party would have to base at Culpeper, the nearest town on a hard road. After a restless night in a nondescript red brick hotel near the railroad station, the party got under way on a Sunday morning, finally getting fairly near the mountain on the south. A faint logging trail led to the base, after which it was a matter of crashing through the brush, clear to the top. The return trip was made via the horseback trail.

Subsequently, a new route via Nethers was figured out by Myron Avery, and on February 22nd, 1929, a tremendous expedition was taken up the mountain by Tom Griffin and the writer. The group, numbering over 70, spent the preceding night in Sperryville, filling every tourist home for miles around, as well as the old hotel run by Eva Browning.

This was the largest excursion ever sponsored by the PATC up to that time. Several came from as far as New York, including Rosemary Brandenburg and Carolyn Buckwell, now Mrs. Glaser. George Keneipp, now Traffic and Safety Director for the District of Columbia, was a guest, and his wife won a certificate for being the first lady to arrive on the summit of Old Rag. Certificates were given to all those making the trip. They were certified by Postmaster William A. Brown, of Old Rag post office.

Glasers with Postmaster

After this expedition, several parties explored around the summit, and some hardy souls even camped on top. It was several months before water was discovered on the summit, and at least two years before Helen Burton* and Egbert Walker charted the famous Ridge Trail in 1934, which is now a popular objective of hundreds of hikers.

So popular has Old Rag become, that the entire tenor of the adjacent country has changed. Several prominent families have taken summer residence on nearby farms. The town of Nethers now greets hiking parties as a routine experience, rather than with the old attitude of distrust and curiosity. Although the town of Old Rag, its post office, stores, and flower-bordered old houses, have vanished and forest now hides the site, a milestone to the progress of Shenandoah National Park. The old mountain, alluring, mysterious and ragged, still stands as a challenge to devotees of the outdoors.

*Helen was courageous enough to ask Frank Schairer, then Supervisor of Trails, for Old Rag as a maintenance job. After looking the assignment over, she asked for some help, and Egbert Walker plus other sturdy hands, volunteered. Egbert was chief cartographer of the enterprise.

The Spectre of the Brocken

October 1935

The Spectre of the Brocken is a phenomenon referred to in mountain-climbing literature as an extraordinary and somewhat terrifying experience to one who beholds it unaware of its meaning. It is an enormously magnified shadow of the observer cast upon a bank of clouds when the sun is low in high mountain regions, reproducing every motion of the observer in the form of a gigantic but mystic image of himself. It was so named, having been first observed on the Brocken Mountain (3,733 feet) of the Harz in Prussian Saxony in Germany.

The most recent of the several accounts of this interesting phenomenon is contained in the 1935 issue of "The Scottish Ramblers' Year Book," extracted from the Cairngorm Club Journal: "On December 28th, 1933, a remarkably clear presentation of the Spectre of the Brocken was seen on Geallaig, the great hill mass lying between the Gairn and Dee beyond Ballater. The hill was under deep snow, and the writer made the ascent from Glen Gairn, following the course of the Milton Burn. The sky was cloudless, and the low winter sun rendered the air mild and warm, so mild indeed that lying on the snow did not give one a sensation of chill. By the time the summit ridge was reached about 11 a. m., mist was rising out of the valleys on both sides and travelling down towards Ballater. The writer was walking in an easterly direction, and was conscious of an accompanying figure on his left. At first little attention was paid to this, as it frequently happens that when on the hill he has a feeling he is not alone, but on this occasion this sensation was more pronounced and persistent, and, on glancing to the left, he was astounded to see a figure about twenty feet high keeping pace some distance away. It was a distinct shock, until it was realized what the figure meant. When the low sun pierced the mist rising from the Dee valley, the shadow of the observer was thrown upon the mist out of the Gairn, and when the sun was bright the head and shoulders of the figure were in the centre of a brilliant disc of rainbow colours, while the whole was surrounded by a complete circle of vivid rainbow, the centre of which was the disc, the figure standing on the circumference. When the sunlight lost its intensity, the rainbow colours disappeared and the shadow faded, but the whole showed up again when the sun was unobscured. For some distance, on both sides of the figure, the shadow of the hilltop was outlined in a broad band of rainbow. The presentation lasted for a considerable period, and was a spectacle not easily forgotten."

Gapland: A Ghost on the Trail

by Orville Crowder
April 1934

The prominence of Crampton Gap antedates the white man's time, for when the early German migrants from Pennsylvania passed through the gap to ford the Potomac and settle in Virginia, long before there were any permanent settlements in Frederick County, they were following a well-defined Indian trail up from the Catoctin and down into Pleasant Valley on the west. And when Joshua Campton was born just west of the divide in 1810, the gap had already long borne the family name.

As we tramp the mountain ridge today, it is interesting to recall that this crestline was once a main avenue of the "Underground Railroad". Many a fugitive slave made the same descent into Crampton Gap and hastened on toward the Pennsylvania line and freedom, perhaps only to fall prey to the slave hunters who combed the mountain farther north and lived comfortably on their rewards for captures.

The part played by the gap in the war which ended this unique ridge travel is familiar history. It was the famous "lost order," delivered to McClellan still wrapped about the three cigars, which brought the Federal troops under Franklin to the foot of the gap at noon that 14th of September, 1862 for a portion of the Battle of South Mountain. The Confederate forces, determined to hold the mountain at the three gaps, Turners, Fox's and Crampton, were formed with their right strongly entrenched behind Burkittsville, at the eastern foot of the gap. Forced up into the gap itself, they staged a valiant three-hour stand, but finally fled westward into Pleasant Valley, though not until it was too late for Franklin's forces to bring relief to the surrounded garrison at Harpers Ferry. The Union forces counted 112 killed and 400 wounded in the narrow limit of this battlefield, and Confederate losses were somewhat greater.

Twenty years later, a young man who had followed these armies as a news reporter visited the gap to procure descriptive material for his new novel *Katy of Catoctin*. Before leaving, he purchased all the land in the gap as a site for the home of his dreams. So came George Alfred Townsend, "Gath" of war correspondent and news-column fame, to Crampton.

Townsend, son of an itinerant Methodist preacher of the Eastern Shore, had gone from college into the editorial offices of the Philadelphia Inquirer, and the early days of the Civil War found him, a youth of 21, war correspondent for the New York Herald. The Seven Days Battle on the Peninsula left him with the Chickahominy fever, and there followed a trip to Europe to recuperate, and a return to the states in 1864 for the closing scenes of the war.

His land purchase opened the Golden Age of Crampton Gap. At first a modest house, "Askalon," rose at the roadside. Then as news columns and books brought a steadily increasing revenue, the estate grew. "Gapland Hall" was built in 1890 with walls of three-foot thickness and "Gapland Den," a twenty-room fantasy of architecture, followed in 1895. All are of native stone, with oak and chestnut beams cut from the surrounding timber. Diplomatic society of Washington waltzed away many an evening in the great ballroom of Gapland Den, and the estate was a social Mecca of Washington, Baltimore and New York at the turn of the century.

It is interesting to note that Gath assigned the use of the various buildings to the individual members of his family, the Den for himself, Gapland Hall for his wife, and Askalon for the two children and their nurses and tutors. All dined together, however, and these meals were doubtless select repasts, as Gath had imported a French chef so that his household might provide for its distinguished guests the same fine food they associated with Old World cafes.

In 1896, Mr. Townsend supervised the erection of the prominent Memorial to War Correspondents in the gap. This arch of elaborately symbolical design is the only war correspondents' memorial in the world, and, like all the buildings in the gap, is a somewhat startling piece of architecture. A lower arch in the shape of a horseshoe is surmounted by three smaller arches: Depiction, Description and Photography according to Gath. Carved heads of Electricity and Poetry appear above two shields emblazoned respectively "Speed" and "Heed." Two horses' heads and a statue of Pan complete the design. The names of 52 correspondents of North and South are listed, and it is interesting to note that one of the contributors to the memorial was the famous Henry M. Stanley. Nearby, numerous historical markers supply details of the war story of the gap.

The $100 income which had supported these activities dwindled long before Gath's death, and he lived to see the spot he loved best in the world drain his funds until he was nearly pauperized. Many fine paintings, antiques, and books were sold during these years, yet the estate was being slowly reclaimed by the wilderness for want of money for repairs. In 1914, the owner died, and his heirs, unsympathetic with his dream of a landed mountain estate which would go down through generations of the family, sold the property for a scant hundredth of its half-million cost. The purchasers, after a forlorn attempt to operate an inn, left the property to the mercy of vandals and the encroaching wilderness.

Townsend's books were prominent bestsellers of their day. "The Entailed Hat" and "Tales of the Chesapeake" were among these, and "Campaigns of a non-Combatant" is a delightful collection of a newspaperman's war-time anecdotes. The Gapland Edition of his poems has many references to the ridge now traversed by the Appalachian Trail and interesting photographs of the estate in the days of its glory. But probably of greatest interest to the mountain lover of today is "Katy of Catoctin," with its rich Maryland Civil War background and choice descriptions of trail surroundings of seventy years ago.

And today, strolling about the ruins of this idyllic dream, it is not hard to sense its fascination untouched by vandalism and the years between. Here is the vault where he had hoped to be laid to rest, with its inscription in the same eccentric style, "Good Night—Gath." The iron statue of his Great Dane dog is gone from its sentry-place above the tomb, re-erected near the road when plunderers found it too heavy to carry. The once beautiful chestnut grove has succumbed to the blight. The many rare plants of the gardens have become extinct. Even the Correspondents' Memorial is showing the effects of time.

But still we look out, as Gath so often did, upon the valley vistas to the east and west and wonder whether, after all, there may not be some basis for the stories the valley folk now tell, of the ghost who walks with heavy tread on crumbling floors and dwells alone in the mountain fastness that he loved so well.

Dr. Jean Stephenson, 1942

The Manor of Leeds

by Jean Stephenson
January 1934

The crest of the Blue Ridge from Chester Gap to Ashby Gap has associations with many people famous in our history, not only in colonial times, but of more recent days. All this land was part of the Northern Neck grant which ultimately came to the Barons Fairfax of Cameron. The roll of agents for the Fairfax family includes some of the most noted names in Virginia: Colonel Nicholas Spencer, Colonel Philip Ludwell, George Brent, William Fitzhugh, Colonel Robert Carter (known from his vast possessions and power as "King" Carter), and lastly, William Fairfax and his son, of "Belvoir", the friends of Washington.

Much of the Northern Neck land was sold outright, but a few "Manors" were erected, over which Lord Fairfax, as "Lord of the Manor," retained his rights and privileges. One of' the first of these was the Manors of Leeds, named for Leeds Castle, of Kent, England, the seat of the Fairfax family. Thomas Lord Fairfax came to Virginia in 1736, laid out the Manor of Leeds, had it surveyed by John Warner, and then went back to England. When he returned in 1745, he stayed first with his cousin, William Fairfax, who was his agent, at Belvoir, in what was then Fairfax County. However, he felt that the country was too civilized and as the foxes were getting scarce, he built a new home, Greenway Court, across the mountains in what was then Frederick County, now Clarke County. Here buffalo, elk, deer, bear, foxes, etc., abounded, and here he lived until his death. He had previously granted Greenway Court Manor to his nephew, Thomas Bryan Martin, for a rental, to be paid each Michaelmas, of one buck and one doe, a quaint survival of an old English custom. Now the best fox-hunting country in Virginia is on and to the east of the Manor of Leeds.

The Manor of Leeds contained 119,927 acres between Hedgeman River on the upper side of Carters Run, on the branches of Goose Creek, on the lower side of the Shenandoah River below Happy Creek, including the Blue Ridge between Happy Creek Gap (now Chester Gap) and Ashby's Gap.

In this tract, he leased most of the land usually for the life of the lessee and any other two persons, with the privilege of renewal indefinitely; but some lots were leased for twenty-one years at a yearly rental of one shilling, the lessee to have the land surveyed, to build a house twenty feet long, sixteen feet wide, with a stone or brick chimney, and to plant an orchard of a hundred apple trees thirty feet apart.

Later, other manors were established nearby, one unnamed covering the land from Ashby's Gap to Williams' Gap (now Snickers Gap), and another, Gooney Run Manor, between Gooney Run and Happy Creek. After the Stamp Act agitation, Fairfax evidently foresaw trouble, for in 1767 he conveyed these manors and the South Branch Manor to his nephew, Thomas Bryan Martin, who reconveyed them to him, thus giving him a private title as well as a seignorial title. The seignorial title ceased with the success of the Revolution, but the private title remained good.

After Fairfax's death in 1781, the title of the lands vested in Denny Martin, although there was much controversy over them. One of the decisions that established the jurisdiction of the United States Supreme Court over State Supreme Courts arose out of the Fairfax land cases.

But meanwhile, after the Revolution, land speculation was rife. Everyone was going to make a fortune in lands. Some did, but more lost all they had. Among the most active speculators was Robert Morris, "the financier of the Revolution," whose daughter married James Markham Marshall. The Marshalls lived near Little Cobbler Mountain, and so were familiar with Leeds. About 1793, John Marshall, later Chief Justice, his brother James Markham Marshall, their brother-in-law Raleigh Colston, and General Henry Lee (Light Horse Harry) formed a syndicate to purchase from Denny Martin and the other Fairfax heirs the Manor of Leeds, Gooney Run Manor, the unnamed Manor reaching to Williams' Gap, and certain other lands. The speculation was almost disastrous, as the title was clouded so they could not sell the land, and it was not until 1806 that it was cleared.

Meanwhile, the Marshalls had become heavily involved, and finally, against his inclination, John Marshall was forced to accept an appointment in 1797 as one of the envoys from the United States to France. Writing of this, Thomas Jefferson states, "Had he not been appointed minister to France, he was desparate in his affairs and must have sold his estate." He received about $20,000 for his services (an ambassador's services were evidently valued more highly then than now), and with this and other sums he and James raised, he was able to complete the purchase.

When the syndicate divided the property, Raleigh Colston received the unnamed Manor and Gooney Run Manor, James the Winchester lots, and certain non-manorial land, while John Marshall kept the Manor of Leeds. The two peaks of North and South Marshall below Chester Gap commemorate the Marshall association and ownership.

The old name of Chester Gap was Happy Creek Gap, while Manassas was Calmese Gap, called after Marquis Calmes who married the daughter of William Waller. Ashby's was first called "the Upper Thoroughfare of the Blue Ridge," but after Thomas Ashby received land on Goose Creek at its junction with Crooked Run (the present site of Delaplane), and later settled near what is now Paris, it became known as Ashby's Bent, and still later as Ashby's Gap. This Thomas Ashby was a prominent citizen both there and in Frederick County where he subsequently lived. His son, John Ashby, was a noted Indian fighter and bore to the Governor at Williamsburg the dispatches telling of Braddock's defeat and death.

The most distinguished member of the family, however, was Col. Turner Ashby of Civil War fame, who is so graphically described in John Esten Cooke's "Surry of Eagle's Nest," which, although a novel, gives one of the best accounts of the Valley Campaign and the first two years of the Civil War in the Upper Virginia section. Many of the scenes are laid in the country around the Manor of Leeds and elsewhere in Fauquier County.

And speaking of names, it is interesting to realize that Francis Fauquier, for whom the County was named, received his appointment as Governor of Virginia after coming to the attention of the public and government officials as author of a pamphlet, "An Essay on Ways and Means for raising Money for the Support of the Present War without increasing the Public Debts," in which he advocated a graduated income tax, as any tax on wages or on necessaries is always shifted from the laborer to the employer and will ultimately be paid by the consumer. Thus, it is evident that the problems of income tax versus sales tax and tariffs were worrying the government leaders two hundred years ago and that bright young men were suitably rewarded then as now. But little did he dream that he would be remembered chiefly because of the county named for him and its fame as the fox hunting country of Virginia.

Why Is It Called That?

by Jean Stephenson
April 1938

The two questions most frequently asked along the Trail are, "How far is it?" and "Why is it called that?" The Guidebook answers the first; it would take a volume almost as big as the Guidebook to answer the second, for it is asked about everything, the counties through which the Trail passes, the mountains, the gaps, the watercourses, the springs, and every place that has a name.

The names are, of course, readily classified into the two groups of names taken from persons and names descriptive of the object or place itself, but that answer is not sufficient. The next inquiry is as to who the person was, if he ever lived there and when, or how long the place has been so described.

The names of the persons form an epitome of history of the region. They range from that of the royal couple who had just become parents of the future George III and who were commemorated in 1738 by having the new counties of Frederick and Augusta named for them, to some of our own group. The county names are interesting in that they show the changing loyalties of the passing decades. After the royal couple followed a series of Royal Governors, Albermarle, Loudoun, Berkeley (Lord Betetourt), Fauquier, all of whom were distinctive characters and merit a longer notice than bare mention of their names. It was after independence was declared that the leader of the opposition party in England was honored by having the new county of Rockingham designated by his name. Among the Revolutionary heroes was John Page of Virginia, whose services were too numerous to mention here; General Joseph Warren of Massachusetts, whose death at Bunker Hill, General Howe declared, off-set the loss of 500 British soldiers; General Nathaniel Greene of Rhode Island, whose services were second only to Washington and whose southern campaign paved the way for Yorktown; George Rogers Clarke, the hero of Vincennes; and James Madison, whose services in the cause of the Constitution have been overshadowed by the fact that he was the husband of Dolly. Rappahannock, of all the Virginia counties we are discussing, is the only one to bear an Indian name. The counties were named for well-known characters of history, but those less known to history are also remembered in the hills.

Snickers Gap takes its name from Edward Snicker, a prominent member of the vestry of Frederick Parish, who was licensed to operate the Ferry across the "Shanandore" before 1764.

Walkers Spring received its name quite recently, from having been rediscovered by Egbert H. Walker, for some years the Trail Overseer for the section between Mt. Weather and Ashby Gap and now the indefatigable chairman of the Maps Committee.

Ashby Gap was so-called because Col. John Ashby, a famous Indian fighter, settled there in colonial days. Among his numerous descendants was General Turner Ashby of the Confederate Army, a distinquished cavalry officer and unusual personality who is graphically described in John Esten Cooke's romance of the War between the States, *Surry of Eagle's Nest*. Ashby's Tavern, which was just west of the crest, was long a landmark of the region and a popular resort in stage-coach days.

Among the most interesting names are those that remind us of the wildlife once so plentiful in the Virginia Blue Ridge, such as Elk Wallow, Bear's Den, and Buck Mountain.

It is also interesting to notice how some names have changed with the changing generations and others have remained the same. John Skinner acquired land running from the crest of the Great Pass Mountain (now Mary's Rock) and down the hollow leading up to Thornton Gap. In his deeds, it is designated as "Skinner's Bower." A generation later, it was divided. The part on the mountain is now "Skinner Ridge." The portion across the hollow became successively "The Bower," "The Bower Farm," "Bower," "the Bowen tract," "the Bowen farm," and finally "the old Bowen place." One is told, in all seriousness, of a Bowen who lived there, and his exploits; actually there was never such a person. It shows how important it is to go to contemporary records for information.

Sexton Knoll traces its name directly to Trail Club activities, being derived from Sexton Shelter, the gift of Dr. Roy Lyman Sexton and Mr. Thomas P. Hickman. While Sexton Shelter has been rebuilt in the George Washington National Forest, the name of Sexton clings to the Blue Ridge. Who knows but that some day Dr. Sexton and Egbert Walker will become legendary heroes of the mountains and much research will be devoted to tracing their exploits!

The Rapidan shows the regard of the colonists for Queen Anne. River after river was named for her, the Fluvanna (the upper James was once so-called), the Rivanna, the North Anna, the South Anna, and the Rapid-Anne (or Rapidan).

Robertson River was not actually so named by Spottswood's Golden Horseshoe expedition, but Robertson, who was a member of it, returned and took up land there and gave it its name. Of the streams named by Spottswood's party, two can be identified today as being called by the names then given, "Mine Run," because there was an appearance of a silver mine by it, and "Mountain Run." Both are far east of the Blue Ridge. Some like to think that the "White Oak" of Spottswood was our White Oak Canyon, but it is unlikely. However, John Fontaine's report of their journey on that day is interesting:

2nd Sept. At nine we were all on horseback and after riding about five miles we crossed Rappahannoc River, almost at the head, where it is very small (meaning Rapidan). We had a rugged way; we passed over a great many small runs of water.... Several of our company were dismounted, some were down with their horses, others under their horses and some thrown off. We saw a bear running down a tree, but it being Sunday, we did not endeavor to kill anything. We encamped by a small river we called White Oak River and called our camp Taylor's camp.

3rd. About eight we were on horseback and about ten we came to a thicket so tightly laced together that we had a great deal of trouble to get through; our baggage was injured, our clothes torn all to rags and the saddles and holsters also torn. About five of the clock we encamped almost at the head of James River (the Rivanna) just below the great mountain. We called

this camp Colonel Robertson's camp. We made all this day
but eight miles.

Few Indian names have survived, probably because the Indians
did not live on the mountains, or because they had retreated before
the encroachments of the whites. So places were called for the white
settlers. These settlers have gone; usually but little can be learned
about them, but
"Their names are on the mountain-side,
Ye cannot wash them out."

Allegheny Horizons

October 1936

Dear Myron:

A certain song, better known to people who attend church on Sundays than those who go to the hills, starts thus:

"There's a land that is fairer than day,

And by faith we can see it afar."

On Memorial Day I saw a portion of the outdoors that seemed to fit this description well. Many would not see it that way. Perhaps it would appear fair only to those who have the mountains so filling their minds that they spill over into their hearts.

The number of such persons is not small. In the particular province of the promised land I wish to tell you of, one does not see by faith as the song says. It is better seen by climbing Wallace Peak and venturing up the steel ladderway of the fire tower thereon.

Some of the place names in this region seem almost to belong in the land of make believe. You have heard of the Little Calfpasture, the Great Calfpasture, the Cowpasture, and the Bullpasture Rivers. It also is the place where the little valleys are "drafts." One little run is called the "Jerkemtight." Then, very small in size but mighty in euphony, is Tizzle Branch; it makes one wonder if there may not have been a Hezekiah Tizzle somewhere in the dim past.

There is an interesting tale about how the Pasture Rivers came to be so named. It is said that the Indians once had stolen a herd of settlers' cattle and were driving them westward into the mountains. The calves naturally tired first; they were left behind at the river which is now the Calfpasture. The cows were driven on farther, but they, too, had to be abandoned; the valley in which they were left became the valley of the Cowpasture. The bulls, being somewhat hardier, were still able to continue westward; they finally were left at the river which we know as the Bullpasture. Our learned historian, Miss Stephenson, has been unable to verify the ancestry of this story. She has found references to the Cowpasture River, by that name, dating back to

1727. A name that old naturally becomes very difficult to trace. If the story is untrue, it represents a high quality of inventiveness on someone's part. I see little point to letting mere veracity stand in the way of a good yarn.

From Elliott Knob one can see a mountain whose crestline runs like a taut, level string for a distance of six miles. On the map, a single 100-foot contour loop, averaging about 500 feet across, encloses the entire six-mile stretch. As Mr. Ramsey of the Calfpasture remarked, the whole top of that mountain is nowhere wider "than from here to the barn." (Reference for Doubting Thomases: U.S.G.S. Map of Virginia, Staunton Quadrangle.)

The following incident will show you the kind of quiet, leisurely people who live in the country. As we were driving, we saw a briskly burning forest fire on a wooded knob near the road. It seemed worth reporting. We stopped at the warden's station to inform the warden of it. He was dressed up, evidently for church. We took him back to the scene of the fire. He decided it "looked bad" and thought the CCC camp should be notified. On our way back to the phone at his farm, he asked us to stop at a farm beside the road. The fire was just around the knoll, so evidently the folks ought to be warned. We should be pardoned if we felt a little bit akin to Paul Revere at this point. The warden called to the woman in the yard; she came and leaned on the whitewashed picket fence. The ensuing conversation went about like this:

"How are you today, Mis' Myrtle?"

"Oh, tol'able, tol'able."

"And how are you, Mist' Smith?"

"Tol'able, tol'able."

"And how is the family?"

"Tol'able."

Then ensued a minute or two of small-talk about the dry weather and the crops. Finally, our friend worked around to mentioning the fire. The conversation then ended and we drove on, the Paul Revere feeling now quite gone.

These, I think, are a mighty fine people. We outsiders were feeling a bit bothered about it all, as though an extra five minutes would result in complete ignition of the countryside. They had a sense of the true proportion of things. They were not discarding habits of quiet speech and courtesy and becoming all wrought up because of a mere fire. On our return from Wallace Peak, we found the fire still doing "tol'able."

Wallace Peak, on Shenandoah Mountain, required a five-mile walk from the road over somewhat stony trail. The path follows up one of the streams feeding into Jerkemtight Run. Some of the rhododendron were in bloom.

Should you ever climb Wallace Peak, I suggest that you carefully save the westward view until the last. To the south, as I recall, the terrain is relatively gentle. Eastward, you see Great North Mountain, with Elliott Knob, and glimpses of the valley beyond. The view to the north is more complex, but you are looking in the direction the ridges run and there is no trouble picking them out. To get a full measure of the western view, you should climb a flight or two of the ladderway up the fire tower; this puts you above the nearby trees.

Below you are the valley of the Cowpasture, backed by Tower Hills Ridge and Bullpasture Mountain. You can make out the gap between these two where the Bullpasture River flows. Then your eyes range into the distance. You see a wild tangle of interlacing mountains that bewilders you. The map has names for them all, and there are dozens of them. There are so many, though, and they link into such a fine pattern, that you soon give up trying to pick them out. (This time Doubting Thomases are referred to the Monterey Quadrangle.) After the westward view, your eyes turn back to the other cardinal points with something like relief.

If the Trail Club is to remain true to its first love, the Blue Ridge, something will have to be done about this siren land. Natural erosion will wear it away eventually, but the time required would be too long for all but the most leisurely of us. One might, of course, greatly accelerate the process of erosion by pasturing sheep all over the mountains. As a temporary expedient, it might be possible to bribe the Geological Survey to destroy all maps of the region: anyone venturing into it would then doubtless become lost and never return. A few such examples should deter all but the most heedless ones. Could it be arranged, the best solution might be to have the region declared unconstitutional by the Supreme Court. That seems to be a standard procedure these days for disposing of things that are unconventional, as this land is. Meanwhile, it exists as a very potent menace to our Blue Ridge allegiance.

I do not believe the picture is overdrawn. If I mistake not, Otis Gates has, indeed, ventured into this territory and still he does wonderfully well by the Blue Ridge. A large part of the council recently became quite wrought up over the much less noteworthy mountains to the north of these. I recall that you yourself became positively lyrical over Reddish Knob. I fear for the same group should it get into this southern country. It would be like giving Swedish punch to people who have known nothing stronger than soda-water or mountain-dew.

That last statement will no doubt cause certain uncharitable ones to question the strength of my own drinking water. I refuse to be troubled by such unkind suspicions. It was indeed powerful country. If some of its potency distilled into its waters, that is no fault of mine.

Sincerely,
Pete

PATC Today

Potomac Appalachian Trail Club

by Aaron Watkins
2003

The Potomac Appalachian Trail Club (PATC) is a volunteer organization with more than 7,000 members. Based in Washington D.C., PATC volunteers are responsible for the maintenance and improvement of nearly 1,000 miles of hiking trails, 30 shelters and 28 cabins in Virginia, Maryland, West Virginia, Pennsylvania and the District of Columbia.

Several of PATC's original members were leaders in the creation of the Appalachian Trail. They met with Federal and State Agencies as well as locals along the corridor to secure land from Maine to Georgia, and they escaped the daily stress of their lives with work trips to clear and map the path. Their commitment created a lasting legacy.

More than 75 years later, the club is responsible for the upkeep of 240 miles of the Appalachian Trail, a stretch which through-hikers often praise as the best maintained, blazed, and mapped anywhere on the AT. The club maintains more than 730 additional miles of trails in local, state, and national parks and forests. In fact, PATC maintains over 80% of the trails in Shenandoah National Park in Virginia, a fact that surprises many visitors.

Members serve, and are part of, an active hiking and backpacking community, with a number of ways to share their love and enthusiasm for the outdoors. Trail maintenance trips and backpacking courses provide opportunities to meet people with similar interests and to develop outdoor skills. Cabin rentals provide a place to retreat with friends and family. Individuals and couples often volunteer as corridor monitors and trail overseers, taking personal ownership for a stretch of wilderness that everyone can enjoy. Climbing and ski sections provide a variety of opportunities for outdoor-lovers with broader athletic interests.

A select group of members participate in PATC's Trail Patrol and

Shenandoah Mountain Rescue Group (SMRG). The Trail Patrol is available in the backcountry to assist hikers and backpackers and to provide information on trail routes and conditions. Shenandoah Mountain Rescue Group is a semi-professional group of volunteers dedicated to wilderness search and rescue and outdoor safety education. SMRG's members assist local authorities in mountain rescues whenever called upon.

A land management and acquisition program is part of PATC's long-term commitment to the protection of the AT. Thousands of acres along the AT corridor are forever protected due to PATC efforts.

The club keeps the public informed of trail conditions and club activities through its web site, maps, and publications. The PATC Web site posts resources for planning upcoming adventures, learning about the history of the region, and interacting with outdoor-lovers from our region and around the world. An interactive trail forum provides a place to chat about your experiences and seek answers to questions. PATC books and maps can be ordered via a secure on-line transaction.

The PATC provides maps of the entire geographic area we maintain, covering approximately 1,000 miles of trails in high detail. The majority of maps are GPS-compatible and contain elevation profiles to provide an additional perspective of possible hikes.

Publications include guidebooks to all of the most popular regional hiking destinations: Old Rag Mountain, Shenandoah National Park, and the Great Falls of the Potomac; and they cover less-travelled areas like the Massanutten Mountain Range, Great North Mountains and the Tuscarora Trail. PATC publishes the Appalachian Trail Club's official guides for the AT in Maryland, West Virginia, and northern Virginia. The club also publishes a catalog of non-fiction books, chronicling local history, identifying wildflowers, and uncovering the origins of the Appalachian Trail.